FRUITS AND BERRIES

The American Horticultural Society
Illustrated Encyclopedia of Gardening

FRUITS AND BERRIES

The American Horticultural Society
Mount Vernon, Virginia

For The American Horticultural Society

President
Dr. Gilbert S. Daniels

Technical Advisory Committee
Everett Conklin
Mary Stuart Maury
Dr. John A. Wott

Fruits and Berries Staff for The Franklin Library/Ortho Books

Editorial Director
Min S. Yee

Supervisory Editor
Lewis P. Lewis

Editor
Ken Burke

Associate Editor
Peter L. Wilkie

Art Directors
John Williams
Barbara Ziller

Creative Director
Michael Mendelsohn

Assistant Creative Director
Clint Anglin

Contributing Editors
Annette Fabri
Kenneth C. Faust
Will Kirkman
James K. McNair
Scott Millard
A. Cort Sinnes

Research Editors
Martha Baker
Lance Walheim

Illustrations by
Ron Hildebrand

Production Director
Robert Laffler

Production Manager
Renee Guilmette

Production Assistant
Paula Green

For Ortho Books

Publisher
Robert L. Iacopi

For The Franklin Library

Publisher
Joseph Sloves

Consultants

Harry J. Amling
Joseph D. Norton
Henry P. Orr
Raymond L. Self
Auburn University

Claron O. Hesse
H. P. Olmo
Perley Playne
Robert G. Platt
University of California

Alec Hutchinson
Horticultural Institute of Ontario, Canada

W. M. Mellenthin
University of Oregon, Mid-Columbia Experiment Station

Robert A. Norton
Northwestern Washington Research and Extension Unit

Fay Paquette
Camarillo, California

Robert D. Way
New York State Experiment Station at Geneva

Major Photography by
William Aplin
Clyde Childress
Michael Landis
William Reasons

Additional Photography by
(Names of the photographers in alphabetical order are followed by page numbers on which their work appears. R = right, C = center, L = left, T = top, B = bottom.)

Josephine Coatsworth
11, 54, 141

Colour Library International
21, 39

Derek Fell
87C,B, 88, 89B, 90B, 103B, 104T,C, 107B, 109R(T to B), 110R,L, 111R, 112T, 115, 119B, 120(all except T), 122C,B, 123R(CT,CB,B), 134B, 135T,B

Pamela Harper
107TR

John M. Lund
27

Michael McKinley
31

Ortho Photo Library
32TL, 33T, 34, 37, 46, 57, 79, 91R, 98, 104B, 105B, 133, 136B

The cover photograph shows a basket of freshly picked strawberries, which can just as easily be grown on a city terrace as in a suburban backyard or country field. Photograph copyright © 1976 by Doris G. Schleisner.

A Special Message from
The American Horticultural Society

Few subjects better deserve the gardener's attention than fruits and berries. The glory of the mature cherry or apple tree in bloom is, after all, matched only by the sweetness of its fruit. The American Horticultural Society is delighted to offer this unique volume, which we hope will convince even a hesitant home gardener that no matter what the growing season or available space, beautiful and satisfying fruit is a goal within reach of all.

In this book you will learn how fruit is planted and cared for, and how to encourage these vital first steps in your own fruit garden. Climate, so much a factor in all gardening, also plays an important role in the successful growing of fruits and berries, and a special effort has been made to describe the effects of climate with simple diagrams and easy-to-read maps. And while no one book could describe in detail the wide variations of climate that exist across the country, attention is drawn in the text and accompanying maps to broad zones where particular fruits and berries are likely to prosper. You will learn which fruits can best survive cold and which cannot; which are disease-resistant in a particular climate and which are not; and, not least important, which are inadvisable for particular climates.

Fortunately, a satisfactory alternative to outdoor planting does exist. The indoor gardener has access to numerous dwarf fruit trees that, when planted in containers, provide valuable flexibility and an almost unlimited choice of fruit. In addition to permitting fruit to be grown outside its recommended climate zone, containers can be placed in a variety of settings, from windowsill to terrace, and good fruit can be grown in very small spaces. Within these pages you will find all the necessary information on container soils, potting and repotting procedures, and how best to feed and water your container-grown fruit trees.

Guided each step of the way throughout the planting and growing process, the home gardener can eagerly look forward to enjoying the beauty and satisfaction of mature fruit. Whether one is interested in any of the common fruit trees—cherry, plum, peach, or apple, for example—or in the wide variety of either cane or bush berries, a large number of nutritious and beautiful fruits are available to the home gardener. And all of them can be grown in limited space. Our suggestions for the pruning and training of such mature plants will result in plants that are of manageable size and will further reward the gardener with more abundant fruit.

The American Horticultural Society recommends this book to two groups of readers: to those who have never grown fruit and would like to begin, and to those experienced fruitgrowers who are looking for ways to increase their crops or add variety to their gardens. This valuable book deserves a place on your gardening bookshelf—just as fruits and berries deserve a place in every garden.

Gilbert S. Daniels
President

CONTENTS

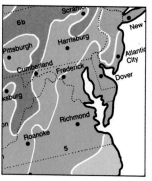

Fruit in Containers 30

Any plant can be successfully grown in containers, which vary widely in size and style, and which offer important mobility to fruit gardeners. Plastic, metal, clay, and wood are commonly used container materials, but the final choice may depend on plant size. This chapter focuses on preparing container soils, potting and repotting procedures, and maintaining containerized fruit.

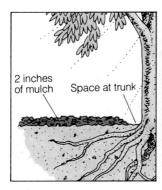

2 inches of mulch   Space at trunk

Codling moth

Planting and Care 38

The satisfactory performance of any fruit plant requires good care. Here you will learn how fruit plants produce, how they grow, and what you need to know to get them started and keep them healthy and productive. Detailed attention is given to common fruit pests and diseases, and what can be done to minimize their effects.

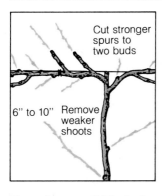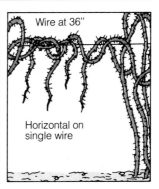

Cut stronger spurs to two buds

6" to 10"   Remove weaker shoots

Wire at 36"

Horizontal on single wire

Pruning and Training 56

Pruning is the most effective means to avoid trouble, improve performance, and maintain healthy plants. This chapter not only outlines which tool to use, how to make a cut, and which pruning methods are best for which trees, but also describes the training of dwarf trees so that they will produce well in confined spaces. Directions are given for both natural and formal shapes.

Encyclopedia of Fruits and Berries 78

This chapter offers valuable listings of the most popular fruit and berry cultivars. Details are given for specific plants in matters such as plant size, hardiness, pest and disease control, and the favorite uses for the fruit once it is harvested. Further information is provided as to which cultivars are best suited for the climates of various geographical regions.

FRUITS AND BERRIES

INTRODUCTION

Dwarf trees make growing fruit in small spaces possible and rewarding. No gardener should overlook the possibility of including fruit.

Strictly speaking, a *fruit* is the seed-bearing portion of any plant, but the term commonly refers to those fruits people eat—crisp apples, pears, peaches, plums, and sweet berries of all kinds. These are the fruits that are the subject of this book. Here you'll find all the most popular fruits and berries suitable for growing by the home gardener. In addition, many of the best varieties for all parts of the country are given, with a description of their important characteristics and their cultural requirements.

Many gardeners share a common misconception about growing fruit, that getting a good crop requires the knowledge and skill of the expert orchardist. Commercial fruit trees do require extensive maintenance and culture, but such efforts are designed to maximize commercial production. The home gardener is not obliged to carry out the complicated spray programs, feeding schedules, or the degree of pruning needed to guarantee commercial success. Modern horticulture has given us improved varieties with better fruiting, better disease resistance, and greater tolerance of many special soil and climate conditions. Your chances of growing good fruit are greater today than ever before. To make the most of them, be sure to learn about your specific growing conditions, and choose the varieties that fit them.

The climate section beginning on page 20 gives valuable information on your part of the country and on how the fruits and berries in this book will perform there. Special requirements for the plants can be found under the individual plant entries in the "Encyclopedia of Fruits and Berries," beginning on page 78. Beyond choosing the best varieties for your area, the amount of attention and care you invest in your plants is up to you. Starting on page 38, there is information on planting, general care, and maintenance.

Fruits in the Landscape

Gardeners who grow fruits and berries at home will tell you that the taste of fruit picked fresh from the tree, bush, or vine is more than enough reason to grow it; but fruit plants today also have an especially important role in enhancing the landscape—even in the small yard or garden.

Until recently, a gardener with an average-size lot had to be content with very little in the way of fruit—perhaps a single apple tree in the center of the lawn and, if lucky, a grapevine growing over an outbuilding or arbor. One fruit tree took up so much space and blocked out so much sun that valuable ground beneath it was too dark to grow lower-growing plants. But even as space has continued to shrink and the average lot has grown smaller, modern horticulture has met the challenge: Fruit trees are available in a range of sizes that permits using them almost anywhere, even in the smallest yards and gardens, and in many other ways as well—spotted about the yard, along the perimeter, as ground covers, or even as small

What Is a Dwarf Tree?

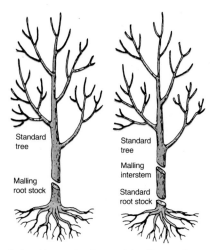

A dwarf tree actually consists of two or three trees. In one type of dwarf, the Malling tree provides the roots, and the standard apple tree provides the fruit. In another type of dwarf, a full sized tree provides the roots, a portion of a Malling tree provides a section of the trunk (interstem), and the standard tree provides the fruit.

shade trees. Modern dwarfing techniques and simplified methods of training allows as many as a dozen fruit trees in the same small garden without sacrificing the sun and light for other fruits, vegetables, or flowers.

Because of these possibilities, this book encourages growing fruits in small spaces. This first chapter focuses on dwarf fruit trees. On pages 56–76 we offer two techniques for keeping fruit plants compact and productive: pruning and training. Growing fruit plants in containers is another effective means of keeping them to size; pages 30–37 present information on healthy and productive container culture, and the "Encyclopedia of Fruits and Berries," beginning on page 78, lists many dwarf varieties best suited to your garden.

Dwarf Trees and the Garden

The key to good fruit in the home garden is in the effective use of dwarf fruit trees. They can not only provide good fruit but also extremely attractive forms, foliage, and flowers.

The value of dwarf trees can be readily appreciated when you consider what would happen to your gardening space if you planted a standard-size apple tree, which can easily reach anywhere from 20 to 40 feet in height, with a 30- to 45-foot spread. Compare this with dwarf apple varieties that can be held to a height of around 10 feet, with a similar spread. Standard apricots, peaches, and plums can grow to 30 feet tall with a similar spread; sweet oranges to 20 to 30 feet tall with a 15- to 20-foot spread; limes to 20 feet tall; and pears to a towering 45 feet with a spread as wide as 30 feet. Dwarf varieties of these trees can be kept to a height of around 10 feet—and in certain cases, even smaller.

'Bonanza' genetic dwarf peach provides a fruitful harvest. The tree will remain small due to its genetic structure.

Natural dwarfs. Dwarf trees are produced in nature or through horticultural practices. Natural dwarfs are called *genetic dwarfs*. Among apples, the most common genetic dwarfs are those known as "spur-type" apples, so named because on the same amount of wood they produce more fruiting spurs than ordinary apple trees. Fruit production has a dwarfing effect because it uses energy that would otherwise go into the growth of the tree. The heavier crops of spur apples slow the tree's growth even further.

Such natural mutations occur with many varieties of apple trees. There are, for example, several spur-type varieties of the popular 'Red Delicious' apple, available to gardeners under such names as 'Redspur' and 'Starkcrimson'. Spur apples grow more slowly than the ordinary trees, but do eventually reach about three-quarters of the normal size; this may be as much as 15 to 30 feet tall with a similar spread—still a large tree for many home gardens. However, they—and indeed all genetic dwarfs—can be made smaller by grafting them to dwarfing rootstocks.

An example of a genetic dwarf apple that is not a spur type is the variety sold as 'Garden Delicious'. It bears fruit resembling the popular 'Golden Delicious' apple, but reaches only 6 or 8 feet in height, and in a container may be kept to a remarkable 3 feet tall.

Genetic dwarf trees can be found among apricots, sweet cherries, sour cherries, peaches, nectarines, and plums. There are several good, extremely cold-tolerant genetic dwarf sour cherries, all of which grow to perhaps 10 feet under ideal conditions but most often stay at 6 or 7 feet tall. Among peaches there is a wide range of genetic dwarfs, all of which grow slowly to 8 or 9 feet. As these have almost no stem between leaves, they have a typically dense or lumpy look. They, along with dwarf nectarine (the nectarine being a *sport*, or mutant, of the peach), are all quite decorative, with large, showy flowers. They are, however, also fairly tender, and tolerate little cold. Many natural dwarfs occur among plums, but these are not plants that bear the popular varieties; rather, they are crosses with western sand cherry, or true cherry, and the shrub plum. Most are readily available in northern parts of the country and are produced commercially for very cold climates.

Horticultural dwarfs. There are several horticultural methods of producing dwarf trees, all of which work by limiting the supply of nutrients to the tree to retard growth. These techniques include pruning, root pruning, girdling and scoring, training, containerizing, and grafting.

Pruning has a dwarfing effect because it removes some of the foliage that enables the plant to grow. Heavy pruning will increase the dwarfing effect.

Root pruning is an effective dwarfing procedure that removes material essential for growth. In this technique, a sharp spade is sunk into the ground around the perimeter of the plant to sever some of the feeder roots.

Girdling and *scoring* also limit tree growth. In girdling, a strip of bark about a quarter-inch wide is removed from around the tree. In scoring, a single cut is made around the tree. Both interfere with the supply of nutrients rising to the top of the tree.

Training, by bending or twisting branches to direct growth, can also have a dwarfing effect. You'll find information about training trees on pages 70–75.

All of these techniques produce only a temporary dwarfing effect and must be repeated periodically. *Growing in containers* can produce a permanent dwarfing by confining the roots of the tree to a small growing space. You must, however, watch to see that roots do not escape from the container and become established in the soil below it.

The easiest and most effective way to produce permanent dwarfing is by *grafting* stems of the desired variety, or *scions*, to dwarfing rootstocks (a rootstock that limits the supply of nutrients). This method offers many advantages to growers, horticulturists, and gardeners, as grafting is the only

A 20-year-old genetic dwarf peach not only bears delicious fruit and takes up little garden space but also has an extraordinary display of flowers each spring.

The small size of the dwarf apple in this patio is maintained by both training and container planting.

Above: 'Red Delicious' scions grafted to a Malling M9 rootstalk produced this dwarf apple, which, after thinning, bore 30 apples in its third year.

Above right: Half barrels are ideal containers for dwarfs such as these 'Southern Sweet' genetic dwarf peaches.

A hedgerow of apples on M9 roots are bent to a 45-degree angle and summer pruned (see page 76) to increase the dwarfing effect of the root.

way to produce large numbers of plants in a relatively short time. It also ensures true reproduction of a desired variety, since seed does not breed true. In addition, grafted dwarf trees will remain uniformly smaller. A secondary effect of grafting is that grafted dwarfs tend to bear fruit at a younger age than the same varieties in standard trees, sometimes bearing fruit as early as the second year.

Grafted dwarfs are readily available at most nurseries and garden centers. More curious, adventuresome, and enterprising gardeners, however, may want to try their own grafting.

Malling rootstocks. The key to producing dwarf trees lies in growth-limiting rootstocks. The most extensive research on dwarf trees has been undertaken with apples. This has resulted in the development, at the Malling Agricultural Research Station in England, of the numbered Malling rootstocks. Since the roots of these special cultivars are relatively shallow and confined in growth, they limit the mature size of any fruit-bearing variety grafted on to them. The illustrations on this page show how rootstocks can be used in two ways to produce dwarf trees. The charts on page 15 show the relative effects of different Malling rootstocks.

Other major fruit trees can also be dwarfed by grafting, but much less research has been done on these. As a result, fewer kinds of dwarfing rootstocks are known, and these are not always as effective as with the apples. Apricots, peaches, nectarines, and plums may be dwarfed on Nanking cherry rootstock; cherries on St. Lucie cherry; and citrus on sweet orange and trifoliate rootstocks. The only reasonably satisfactory rootstock for grafting pears is quince.

Among the advantages to growing dwarf trees is easy care. When the distance from roots to treetop is 10 feet or less, sprays for pests and diseases are easier to apply and pruning is less difficult and time-consuming. Feeding and watering are also easier because roots are shallow and less extensive—you'll end up applying less fertilizer and water and saving more time and money. These advantages become greater if you further reduce size of the trees by applying the appropriate pruning and training techniques offered in this book.

Apple Tree Size Differences

To determine the correct spacing of dwarf trees, you should know the natural size of the variety as well as the dwarfing effect of the rootstock. The two charts will help you make this determination.

For instance, the 'Red Prince Delicious' tree is naturally larger than 'Jonnee'. If grown on the same rootstock, 'Jonnee' can be planted closer together than 'Red Prince'. 'Red Prince' on MM 106 should be planted 14 feet apart, while 'Jonnee'' on MM 106 is planted at 12-foot intervals.

Or, if you are planting them together, 'Jonnee' should be ordered on a larger rootstock to make best use of the spacing needed for the 'Red Prince'. In this case, 'Jonnee' on MM 111 would fit in the same space as the 'Red Prince'.

Rootstock	% of natural size
Malling 9	40%
Malling 26	50%
Malling 7	60%
MM 106	70%
MM 111	75%

'Jonnee'

Actual tree size is determined by local climate and growing conditions. The sizes of these varieties are shown not by feet, but on a relative scale of 100.

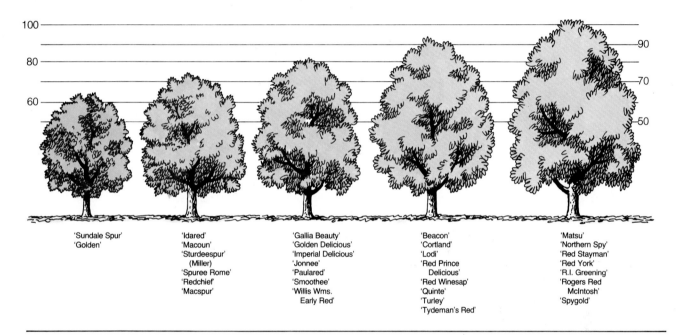

'Sundale Spur'	'Idared'	'Gallia Beauty'	'Beacon'	'Matsu'
'Golden'	'Macoun'	'Golden Delicious'	'Cortland'	'Northern Spy'
	'Sturdeespur'	'Imperial Delicious'	'Lodi'	'Red Stayman'
	(Miller)	'Jonnee'	'Red Prince	'Red York'
	'Spuree Rome'	'Paulared'	Delicious'	'R.I. Greening'
	'Redchief'	'Smoothee'	'Red Winesap'	'Rogers Red
	'Macspur'	'Willis Wms.	'Quinte'	McIntosh'
		Early Red'	'Turley'	'Spygold'
			'Tydeman's Red'	

The Malling and Merton Malling Rootstock Numbers Determine Tree Size

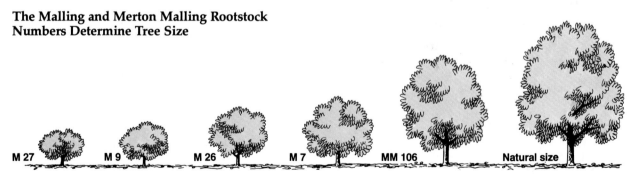

M 27   M 9   M 26   M 7   MM 106   Natural size

M 27—Very dwarfing. Mature trees reach about 4 feet. Hard to find; limited availability.

M 9—Most dwarfing root currently available (about 9 feet). Trunk section and root are brittle, so stake freestanding plants. Try to buy trees with bud 6 inches or more above the crown (where roots branch), and plant with bud 2 inches above soil for extra anchoring.

M 26—Less dwarfing than M 9 (about 12 feet) unless used in formal espaliers, containers. Fewer suckers than M 7.

M 7—Widely available semidwarfing root (about 15 feet). Trees budded high and planted deep will sucker less if you can find them. Suckers may be dug or layered for home grafting. Control size by training, pruning.

MM 106—Largest semidwarfing rootstock (about 18 feet). Trees can reach ¾ of full size. This root anchors well, suckers very little, and resists woolly apple aphid. It is mainly a commercial root stock.

A Fruit Garden

The sample plan on page 19 gives some idea of how fruit plants might be placed in a relatively small area, and illustrates the remarkable space-saving possibilities of gardening with fruit. Notice the orientation of the garden. Fruit needs sun to set a crop, and the illustrated arrangement allows for maximum exposure to the sun as it passes from east to west. If your own location does not have all-day sun, at least plan to give your fruit plants southern or western exposures.

Notice also how this plan makes use of espaliered apple trees, cane berries, and grapevines to provide an attractive border and plenty of fruit, while still allowing space for other plants. The berries are trained on trellises and oriented approximately north and south. These take up little space and bear heavily. The grapes are planted mainly on the north side of the garden to give them full southern exposure to the sun, which is necessary in order to develop good sugar content in the fruit. Note that there is still room in the center of the garden for dwarf fruit trees, raised beds in which to grow vegetables or flowers, a plot of annuals, a good stand of raspberries, and more, without crowding the plants or you.

To show how such a garden might actually be carried out, the photographs on this and the following pages illustrate a garden developed by David Whiting of St. Helena, California, that measures 15 by 50 feet and yet contains 17 fruit trees, several grape varieties, cane berries, ornamental plants, and vegetables. The training of plants plays a most important part in this garden. Instructions for making formal espaliers similar to those in these photographs are on page 75. This requires a little effort; and once established, espaliered trees can be allowed to grow closer together. They will still receive good light, allow perfect air circulation, have plenty of root space, and will require less spraying, fertilizing, and pruning.

These small espaliered apple trees will eventually create a garden wall around a small orchard of dwarf trees.

A dwarf nectarine and a dwarf peach grow beside raised vegetable beds.

Clockwise from below: David Whiting trains one of his 19 grafted apple trees; three dwarf trees in the Whiting garden provide a harvest of three varieties of peaches; espaliered apples line the picket fence; the initial effort in training pays off in healthy trees you can reach easily for care and harvesting.

Above: From the north end of the Whiting garden, the view encompasses many varieties of raspberries in the foreground and dwarf peach and nectarine trees in the background

Right: In midsummer, carrots and lettuce fill the raised beds among the fruit trees.

A Sample Garden

When you landscape with fruit, you combine beauty with practicality. You may not want a garden composed almost entirely of fruit, but would rather add a few fruit plants to enhance your surroundings.

There is a story about a California gardener who was approached and asked about the fruits on his 50-foot lot. After a bit of thought he said, "I guess I don't have much fruit here." It was pointed out that he had a persimmon, a pomegranate, and a fig along the driveway, two dwarf apples espaliered behind some zinnias, a quince in the side yard, orange, lemon, and lime trees outside the bedroom, and a kumquat and a Japanese plum in back. He concluded that yes, he did have a lot of fruit after all.

Overlooking 11 fruit trees on such a small lot may seem like extreme absentmindedness, but this gardener's trees fit effortlessly into the landscape, and required no more care and attention than the flowers or the lawn. Spraying and pruning gradually became part of his regular garden chores, so he never thought of his "orchard" as something special. Such an unobtrusive, harmonious blending of fruit plants into the landscape is a goal worth striving for.

In addition to the ease with which fruit trees can be accommodated in the small garden, fruit trees also serve many functions in the landscape. Apple trees, for example, make superb shade trees anywhere in the yard, and especially over an outdoor sitting area. Be sure to prune them to a branch high enough to allow passage underneath. A large crab apple or a spreading cherry such as the 'Napoleon' variety also will provide good shade.

Any fruit tree you like can be used as a focal point or accent in the yard or garden. The most striking trees in bloom are apples, cherries, quince, and the showier flowering peaches. Crab apples are especially effective. These hardy trees are the most widely adapted of all flowering trees and offer abundant displays of red to pink to white blossoms, followed by brilliantly colored fruit. As a rule they require some winter chilling, but cultivars are available that bloom beautifully, even in the mild Pacific Coast climates. Some crab apples have fragrant blossoms; others have red to purple foliage. Citrus trees, where they can be grown, also have attractive foliage, showy fruit over a long season, and wonderful fragrance.

Shrub fruits can also play an important role in the landscape, either as individual accents, or in hedges or shrub borders. Blueberries and currants can be used, but currants are most effective, with their beautiful flower clusters and bright scarlet fruit.

Genetic dwarf peach trees make splendid flowering hedges, and showy-flowered dwarf or standard peaches can be trained in the same way. With appropriate pruning, apples or pears also will form attractive hedges or borders.

You can even use fruit as a ground cover. Strawberry plants are effective, especially in smaller areas, but plan to replace them every three years with new plants if you want a good fruit crop. For larger areas, use the low-bush blueberry.

These are just a few ideas for planting with fruit. Other possibilities depend upon climate, soil, available varieties, and your own taste. This book will give you the information you need to enjoy all the benefits of gardening with fruits and berries.

The 15 × 50-Foot Sample Garden

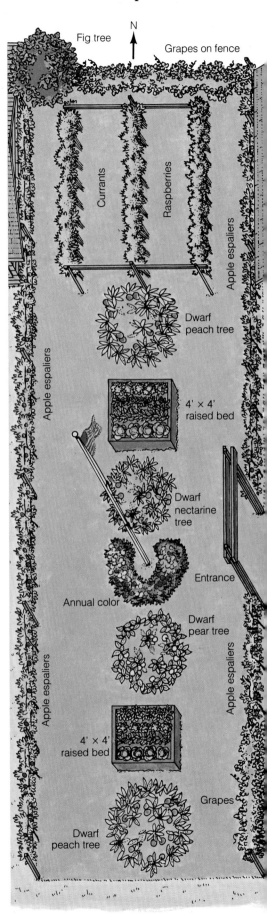

N

Fig tree

Grapes on fence

Currants

Raspberries

Apple espaliers

Dwarf peach tree

4' × 4' raised bed

Dwarf nectarine tree

Entrance

Annual color

Apple espaliers

Dwarf pear tree

Apple espaliers

4' × 4' raised bed

Grapes

Dwarf peach tree

CLIMATE

Length of growing season and plant hardiness are keys to the successful growing of fruits and berries.

The majority of the fruits discussed in this book are often referred to as *temperate-zone* fruits. The temperate zone in the Northern Hemisphere lies between about 23½ degrees latitude and the Arctic Circle. This, however, tells little about the climatic conditions in which these plants will grow and do well. In the United States alone, the growing season—the period between the last frost in winter and the first frost of the following winter—ranges from 3 to 12 months in length, depending upon location. Climates, and all of the factors that make up climate—prevailing temperatures, humidity, rainfall, cloud cover and fog, amount of sunshine, and winds—vary enormously throughout the country. Furthermore, they vary not only over large distances, between cities and towns, but within cities, from block to block and garden to garden, and sometimes even within the same garden. This is why gardeners in recent years have taken to thinking and planning in terms of *microclimates*. Microclimates are created by local topographical features, by vegetation such as trees and shrubs, and by manmade structures such as fences and houses.

Your own garden may have several microclimates of its own. For example, a spot protected from the wind will have a microclimate warmer than a spot out in the open. If the sheltered spot is backed by a wall that reflects heat, that area will be even warmer. In a northern garden such a location might be ideal for helping a tree bear better fruit, whereas in a southern garden it might produce too much heat.

This extreme diversity of climate in the United States and the possible variations even within individual gardens make it impossible for any gardening book to provide an exact guide to climatic conditions. In this chapter, however, there are some good general guidelines on climate in your part of the country and on what fruits to grow there. This information will help you choose the varieties most likely to do well in your garden. For more detailed information, check with local nurseries, garden centers, agricultural extension agents, and—an especially good source—gardening friends and neighbors who can tell you about their own successes and failures.

Climate Zones

The map on pages 22 and 23 is divided into zones. Each zone takes two factors into consideration: the approximate length of the growing season for fruit plants, and the minimum winter temperature, which determines plant hardiness, or ability to withstand cold.

We have divided the country into three sections: the southern states, the midwestern and northeastern states, and the western states. We have drawn a further distinction between the West and California because of the wider climatic variations within California. The following sections describe the characteristics of the various zones.

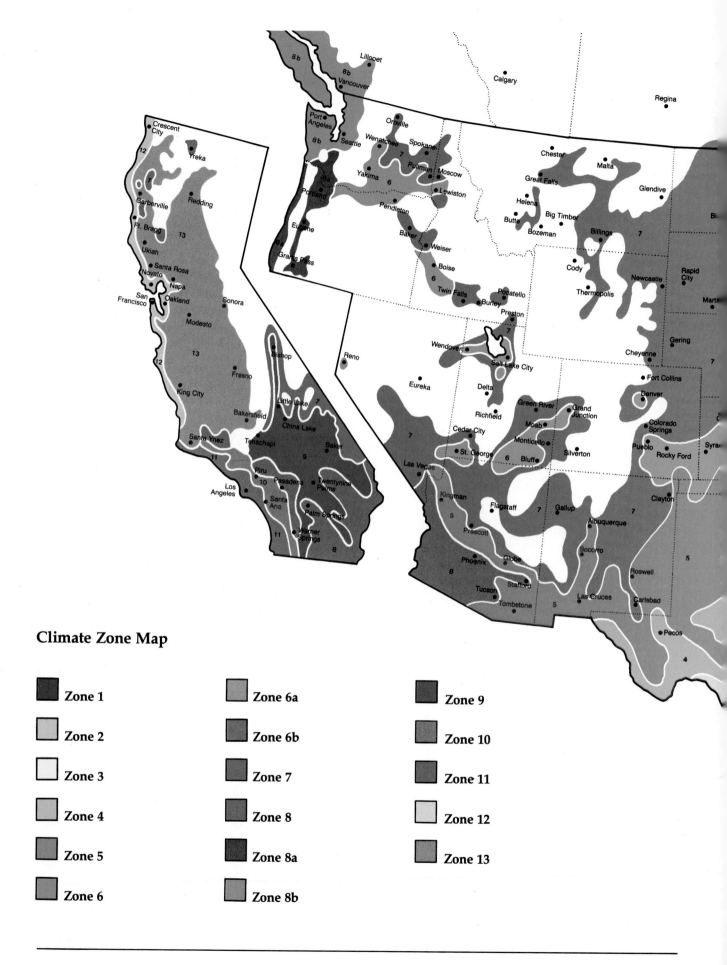

Climate Zone Map

Zone 1
Zone 2
Zone 3
Zone 4
Zone 5
Zone 6

Zone 6a
Zone 6b
Zone 7
Zone 8
Zone 8a
Zone 8b

Zone 9
Zone 10
Zone 11
Zone 12
Zone 13

A period of protective dormancy ends with the longer days and rising temperatures of early spring, which brings a release of buds such as these apple blossoms.

Fruit Climates of the South

The southern states have such a broad range of climates that no rules apply to the whole region. The major winter influence is a mass of cold continental air that moves down from the Canadian plains, sometimes reaching into the usually mild regions of the Gulf Coast and Florida. Severe cold spells seem to occur in the Deep South in cycles of from 10 to 20 years, with less severe spells every 4 or 5 years. The major summer influence is the warm, moist Gulf air, reaching northward and inland, up rivers, and along valleys to affect areas far from the coast.

The South is a favored fruit-growing region, hospitable to a broad range of fruiting plants. However, hot, moist summers favor the spread of pests and disease. The gardener must be especially careful to check plants often, allow for good air circulation, and spray when necessary.

When planning a fruit garden in the South, you will have to determine the variations in climate most common to your specific locality. For example, the gardener in Tennessee or Kentucky may have next to no warming influence, and the certainty of cold winters. Apples and pears will do well. Peach varieties should be chosen on the basis of those requiring a long period of dormancy. Plums and sour cherries will do well, but apricots and sweet cherries may suffer in some years from fall or spring frosts.

The gardener south of Baton Rouge, Louisiana, can plant tender crops such as citrus, but can also count on damage or even loss of the more tender crops on a regular cycle of perhaps every 10 years. These plants can be replaced and bear fruit again within a season or two.

In borderline areas between zones, you may be able to choose from a wide range of fruiting plants, but always with the understanding that damage may occur in winter, and that the hot, moist summer can mean trouble for the hardier plants. You'll want to choose pears that resist fireblight, a bacterial infection that is at its worst in warm spring and fall weather. Peaches should be resistant to leaf spot and canker.

In recent years, breeding stations in the South have developed peach varieties that grow and fruit as far south as Florida. The pear, once limited by fireblight to a few cooking varieties, now includes a wide range of blight-resistant varieties. The territory suitable for bunch grapes has also been extended, and now even Florida gardeners can grow some varieties.

Climate zones of the South. The southern region is divided into six zones. In general, if you live in a northerly or inland portion of a zone your climate will be more severe and your season shorter.

Zone 1. Grow tropical plants in this zone only. Grow citrus and mangoes instead of pears and peaches.

Zone 2. This zone includes the band around the Gulf Coast where citrus and subtropicals can be planted commercially. An occasional freeze may cause damage.

Zone 3. This zone has a strong tropical influence. The hardy subtropicals grow well, but some temperate fruits are limited.

Zone 4. This zone is the upper section of the Cotton Belt. The short winter and long growing season call for varieties that prefer little winter cold. Disease is a problem.

Zone 5. The zone north of the Cotton Belt is hospitable to any temperate-zone fruit, but choose varieties that tolerate cold.

Zone 6. This zone includes mountainous inland areas. The growing season is shorter and winters can be harsh. Use the hardiest temperate fruits, and in winter provide protection such as windbreaks and deep mulching with an additional layer of evergreen boughs.

In the coldest New England regions, apple crops are plentiful.

Fruit Climates of the Midwest and Northeast

The climates of the northern region of the United States range from the harsh winters and short, cool summers of upper Michigan to the fairly mild coastal climates of New Jersey. At least some varieties of fruit will grow in each of these climate zones.

In much of the North, extreme winter cold is a serious threat to fruit. Be sure to choose the hardiest varieties. Much damage from cold depends upon whether the plant is dormant: A completely dormant plant takes cold better than one that has begun to grow again. Flower buds are particularly sensitive to late frosts and freezes. Plant trees where cold air can flow away from the fruit garden, and the change from warm spring days to colder nights is not too severe.

Another northern and midwestern threat is wind, which can dry plants out when ground water is frozen and thus unavailable to the plants. If you have no naturally protected site for planting, put in an evergreen windbreak when you put in your fruit plants. A windbreak of trees is more effective than a solid barrier such as a fence, since the wind won't flow over the top in a solid wave and sweep down onto the other side. For temporary wind protection, use snow fencing or burlap tacked to stakes.

The first strong sun can do serious damage to plants that are still leafless. You may want to protect your trees from sunburn in these situations by wrapping the trunks with burlap and painting the trunk and main branches with white interior latex paint.

Little can be done about ice, but you should be careful to remove snow and icicles if they threaten to build up enough to break branches.

Climate zones of the Midwest and Northeast. The map on pages 22 and 23

Top: Large bodies of water temper harsh Midwest and Northeast weather and create a climate where cherries and other fruits can grow.

Above: Peaches grow in California's interior valleys, along with many other fruits, in one of the nation's richest fruit-growing regions.

divides this region into five zones. If you live in a northerly or inland portion of a zone, your climate will be more severe and your season shorter.

Zone 5. This zone is particularly good for growing fruit. In the mildest coastal areas, gardeners can even try a fig tree in a warm corner.

Zone 6. Fruit crops do well in this area if you protect them from the worst weather. The growing season is long, but occasional extremes can cause damage.

Zone 6a. The presence of large bodies of water in Michigan, Ohio, New York, and coastal New England has a tempering effect on the climates of these areas, making winter less severe and summer longer. This is the case in the fruit belt of the southern portion of Michigan, where commercial orchards produce cherries, peaches, and many other fruits. You can plant any temperate-zone fruit here with good prospects for success, although you will need to plant the hardiest apricots and fairly hardy plums and peaches.

Above: An old peach tree presides over a field of wild mustard in bloom.

Zone 6b. This zone includes the coldest areas of New England. It corresponds to zone 7, but with less severe winds and more snow cover. Apples are among the best tree crops. Give plants protection, and use dwarf trees in containers that can be brought inside in winter.

Zone 7. This zone includes the coldest parts of the United States. The short growing season and late frosts limit fruit plants to the hardiest varieties. In the central states winds can be intense. Windbreaks and other protections are necessary. Consider growing dwarf trees in containers that can be brought indoors for part of the year.

Fruit Climates of the West and California

In the western states there are many prime areas for fruit growing, from the Pacific Northwest to the Salt Lake area and the Arizona desert. There are six climate zones in the West, seven in California. The areas designated by white are considered too harsh for fruit crops.

The Northwest and the mountain and high-desert regions of California are rich berry-producing areas.

Climate Zones of the West

Zone 5. Gardeners in the high desert of Arizona and New Mexico escape the worst summer heat and can grow fine apples, pears, and many other fruits. Cold, however, rules out tender plants.

Zone 6. This zone dots itself around the map. It is cold, but not nearly as cold as the related climate of zone 7. Some influence of terrain (or water, in Utah) lengthens the growing season and tempers the winter. Eastern Washington, for example, is prime apple country, with extensive commercial orchards, but it also produces fine peaches of the high-chill 'Elberta' type, and home gardeners can succeed with almost any temperate-zone crop. For apricots and cherries, try the hardiest varieties.

Zone 7. Related to zone 6, but with a growing season up to 30 days shorter, this is still a mild enough climate for hardy varieties of most temperate-zone fruits. There is commercial fruit production in both Colorado and Montana. Protect trees by mulching the roots heavily in winter, holding the mulch in place with wire. Plant on ground that has good drainage, and establish windbreaks.

Zone 8. In the area of Phoenix, Arizona, the climate corresponds roughly to the low desert regions of California, producing fine grapefruit and mandarin oranges. Temperate-climate fruits such as apples and pears, won't survive here.

Zone 8a. The milder, warmer parts of southern Washington and western Oregon produce much of the nation's sweet cherry crop, fine pears, and quantities of berries. The home gardener can plant almost any temperate-zone fruit, but summers are overcast and cool, so fruits that need heat, like peaches and grapes, must be carefully chosen for the region.

Zone 8b. This zone is similar to zone 8a but with even cooler, wetter summers. It is more important in this zone to be careful in choosing fruits that need less summer heat.

Climate zones for California

Zone 7. This zone includes the high slopes above Owens Valley and the Mojave desert. The growing season of 120 to 160 days permits many fruits, but berries and dwarf trees will need heavy winter mulch to survive without damage.

The sequence of bloom is always the same from year to year (pear blossoms).

Zone 8. The low desert is good for plants that need heat. Winter cold and wind make many fruit plants impossible to grow, and the summer heat rules out apples, pears, and cherries.

Apple trees are also a good choice in the colder zones of the West.

Zone 9. Intermediate and high desert gardeners escape the worst of the summer heat and can grow fine apples and pears and many berries. Cold temperatures rule out tender plants.

Zone 10. This zone includes the hot inland region just behind the Southern California coast. It produces commercial citrus crops. Plants that need heat do well if they can withstand some winter frost.

Zone 11. This is California's subtropical belt, with many commercial groves of avocados. Any citrus will grow in this zone. Surprisingly, the hills just behind the coast are fine for many cool-climate fruits such as apples. Nurseries in the area carry any fruit you're likely to have heard of, and low-chill dwarf peaches grow especially well.

Zone 12. The summer fog belt of coastal California is in many places a prime fruit area. Commercial growers around San Francisco Bay harvest European plums, Oriental plums, apricots, and sweet cherries. The coast north of the Bay may have enough summer fog to affect the ripening of plants that need heat, such as peaches and grapes, so choose the hottest spots in the garden for these.

Zone 13. The interior valleys from the Inner Coast Range to the Sierra Nevada include some of the finest fruit climates of the United States. Commercial orchardists grow peaches, plums, citrus, strawberries, and almost all of California's wine and table grapes grow here. Central Valley heat limits the choice of apples and pears.

These dwarf peaches will stay small enough
to thrive in containers, but will still yield an
abundant harvest.

FRUIT IN CONTAINERS

Containers provide a good growing environment for any fruit, and their mobility offers scope to the gardener's imagination.

At the famed Palace of Versailles in the 1600s, the gardeners of Louis XIV decorated the grounds with many potted orange trees. During the summer the trees lined the walks of the palace gardens; then, when the snows came, the gardeners wheeled them indoors to a special greenhouse, which became known as the *orangerie*. Some of these trees, it is said, lived for 75 years.

Mobility is the principal reason for growing fruit in containers. Moving fruit plants to shelter when cold weather comes, or to a shady spot if excess heat is the problem, makes it possible to grow them outside of their normal climate ranges. Using containers you can relocate plants to where they do best and even try varieties not normally recommended for your climate, such as lemons in Michigan, or peaches in North Dakota. Citrus, in fact, is so attractive in containers that you might consider bringing a small tree into the house for the winter to fill a sunny south window. Deciduous trees would survive a winter season in a garage, if given sun on good spring days. One caution, however: Just because a plant can survive winter in the ground in your area does not mean it can manage cold weather in a container. If your garden soil freezes to any depth at all, container soil is likely to freeze all the way through. Gardeners in the coldest northern zones should plan to protect even hardy deciduous plants during the coldest months of the year.

Choosing Plants

What fruits can you plant in containers? The answer is virtually any ones you like. Trees, of course, must be grafted or genetic dwarfs. The "Encyclopedia of Fruits and Berries" beginning on page 78 lists many dwarf varieties of apples, apricots, cherries, nectarines, peaches, pears, and plums—all suitable for container culture. You can also use citrus, grafted to trifoliate orange rootstock. Any fig can be grown in a container. Strawberries can be planted in large or small containers, and blueberries and currants make excellent container plants. You can even plant spur-pruned grape varieties, or any of the other grape varieties, providing you give them a trellis or other support during the growing season.

Choosing Containers

What kinds of containers are suitable for growing fruit plants? The answer, again, is almost anything you like—as long as it will hold the plant and a sufficient amount of soil, is nontoxic, and contains holes for adequate drainage. Half-barrels, for example, make excellent containers for fruit trees, as shown in the photograph on page 14. Some people even use rubber wastecans, plastic utility containers available at paint stores, or metal lard cans.

Garden centers, nurseries, and other retailers offer clay, ceramic, porous concrete, plastic, and wood containers in many sizes and shapes. Plastic and metal containers have the advantage of holding moisture longer. Clay

dries out quickly, necessitating more frequent watering, and clay pots are comparatively heavier, an important consideration if you move your containers. Wood has several advantages, not the least of which is its light weight relative to its strength. As containers filled with soil can be extremely heavy—soil alone can weigh about 90 pounds per cubic foot when dry, 100 pounds when wet—the lighter wood containers can make a significant difference when you come to relocate them. Another advantage of wooden containers is that they can be made so that their sides are screwed together so that they can be detached easily. This greatly facilitates the occasional root pruning that is necessary (see page 13). Wood is also readily available, and is, therefore, a convenient building material for those gardeners who wish to make containers to their own specifications.

Whatever type of container you choose, the size should be just 2 or 3 inches wider than the roots of your plants. The right size container will let the plant find water and nutrients easily, keep soil from going sour around and beneath the roots, and slow top growth. If you start with a bareroot apple or pear, or one of the genetic dwarf fruits, your first container should be about the size of a 5-gallon can. Let the young tree grow for a season and then repot it the following spring into a larger container. Move plants

Bottom right: An espaliered 'Gravenstein' apple in a wooden planter is decorative and gives a good crop.

Bottom left: A 'Meyer' lemon in a ceramic container bears flowers and fruit year round.

Below: Strawberries grow in a hanging moss basket along with a frosting of sweet alyssum.

from the nursery 5-gallon size container to the bushel size over two or three seasons.

Evergreen fruit plants such as citrus should be started in a container not much bigger than the rootball. If your soil mix has good drainage, you can use a box 3 or 4 inches wider than the roots all around. For large nursery plants—for example, those in 15-gallon cans—the first container may be the permanent container. If you wish to hide the metal can, you can put it in a large basket, or surround it with a box easily fashioned from wood panels.

If you plan to move the plant and its container, carefully consider container size in advance. The maximum for permanent containers should be about bushel-basket size. Anything bigger will be too bulky to handle or move. Half-barrels, or any boxes, or pots that hold an equal volume of soil are roughly the right size. The minimum permanent size should be about 18 inches on a side and 18 inches deep. The smaller the container, the easier it is to move. Keep in mind, however, that the plant must have sufficient room for its roots, and that more work is involved in feeding, watering, and root pruning with smaller containers. All these factors must be balanced when choosing the best container.

Above and below: 'King's Ruby' grapes in a wooden container require frequent attention for watering and feeding. Be sure to provide a trellis for support; here the unusual shape of the wooden containers is accentuated by the corresponding outward shape of the trellis.

Below left: Muscat grapes in a wooden planter are trained on a wood-and-wire trellis.

This strawberry "tree" is a half-cylinder of soil mix held in place by sphagnum moss and wire mesh. Impatiens in the lower half add additional color to the column.

Making Your Own Soil Mix

You can make your own soil mix by using one of the formulas in the text and mixing it very thoroughly. By "very thoroughly" we mean that it must be mixed so each portion, even a 2-inch potful, has the proper portions of each ingredient. To mix it well follow these steps:

1. Pour the dampened peat moss, sand, and ground bark in a rough pile. Sprinkle the fertilizer and lime on top.

2. Shoveling from the first pile, make a cone-shaped pile by pouring each shovelful directly on top so ingredients dribble down the sides.

3. Shovel from the second pile and repeat the cone-shaped pile building and dribbling.

4. Do it again. Make a third cone-shaped pile. It's then ready to use.

Container Soils

Because containerized soil loses moisture easily, it must be of a type that holds moisture well. But to prevent soggy roots and the possibility of disease, it also must have good drainage. Commercial mixes such as Jiffy-Mix and Redi-Earth, often referred to as "soilless mixes," or "synthetic soils," fit the bill. Jiffy-Mix, the most widely available synthetic soil, is made up of 50 percent peat moss and 50 percent vermiculite. It contains enough nutrients to sustain initial plant growth and provides fast drainage, leaving a reservoir of air and water after drainage.

Synthetic mixes offer several advantages: They are free of disease organisms, insects, and weed seeds; they are light in weight—half the weight of garden soil when both are wet—an advantage both in relocating container plants and in growing them on roofs or balconies; and furthermore they can be used just as they come from the bag, without needing to be moistened down for planting, or specially mixed.

If you are planning to fill a number of containers, you may want to save money by mixing your own planting medium. Here are two recipes:

  9 cubic feet of fine sand
18 cubic feet of ground bark or
    nitrogen-stabilized sawdust

or, for a coarser soil,

  9 cubic feet of peat moss
  9 cubic feet of fine sand
  9 cubic feet of ground bark

Add to either of the above:

  5 pounds 5–10–10 fertilizer
  7 pounds ground limestone
  1 pound iron sulphate

Some gardeners like to add a little rich loam to the mix of sand and organic material. Add up to one-third loam, but be careful not to include clay soil, which doesn't drain well. Remember that while adding topsoil to the mix when planting in containers may give the mix good physical properties, it also increases the risk of introducing pests and diseases.

Potting and Repotting

Before you pot up your fruit plant, make sure your container has good drainage. Cover the drainage holes with broken pieces of pot, glass, or crockery, making sure not to cover the holes tightly, which will retard drainage. Do not fill the bottom with rocks or coarse gravel, which interferes with water flow.

To plant a bareroot plant, place enough soil mix in the pot so that when the mix is lightly tamped down, the roots just touch it when the crown of the plant is slightly below the container rim. Hold the plant at that level and add enough mix to support it, tamping lightly as you go. Finish planting by filling the container to about a quarter inch below the rim. The soil will settle, leaving you room to water.

Plants from nursery containers can be placed on the first layer of soil. With these fill in the soil mix around the rootball, but first scratch the rootball all around with a fork to break up roots and direct them outward. Be sure to cut off long spiraling roots at the bottom of the container.

Repotting is performed in a similar manner as shown in the illustrations on page 36. Repotting is necessary because plants tend to bunch feeder roots at the wall of a container, where they dry out faster. This, in turn, creates shortages of water and nutrients, even allowing for proper care. When you shave off an inch of root and add fresh soil, the plant will grow healthy young roots in the new reservoir of moisture and nutrients. Be sure always to clip back the top of the plant when you shave its roots in order to provide a balance between the two. New top growth will soon follow new root growth. After potting or repotting, give the plant a good, deep watering.

Steps in Repotting

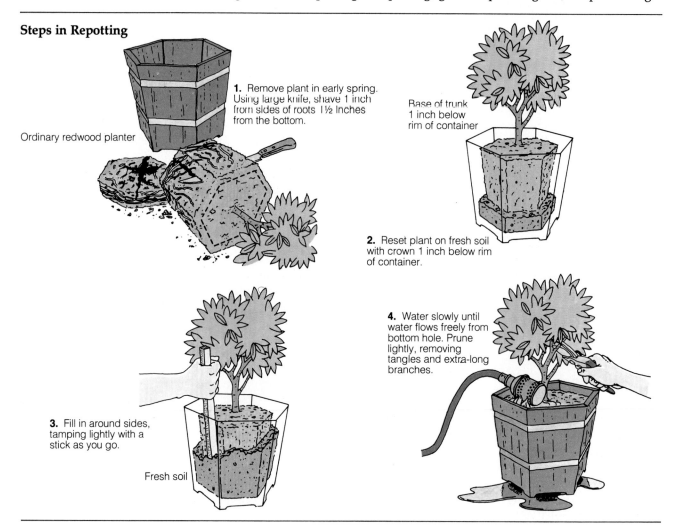

Ordinary redwood planter

1. Remove plant in early spring. Using large knife, shave 1 inch from sides of roots 1½ inches from the bottom.

Base of trunk 1 inch below rim of container

2. Reset plant on fresh soil with crown 1 inch below rim of container.

3. Fill in around sides, tamping lightly with a stick as you go.

Fresh soil

4. Water slowly until water flows freely from bottom hole. Prune lightly, removing tangles and extra-long branches.

Feeding Container Fruit Plants

Use the growth and appearance of the plant as guides to feeding. The plant should leaf out and grow vigorously in the spring and early summer, and leaves should be a healthy medium green. Yellowed leaves suggest a lack of nitrogen, while very dark leaves may indicate overfeeding.

With a purely synthetic soil mix, you should be careful about feeding. The nutrients you add will wash through the soil when you water, so you'll have to feed more often. It's best to keep to a regular schedule.

One good feeding method is to give each plant about half the recommended quantity of complete fertilizer (one that contains nitrogen, phosphorus, and potassium) every 2 or 3 weeks. A liquid fertilizer is easier to measure in exact proportions, and is also less likely to burn roots. If the label recommends 1 tablespoon per gallon of water each month, use 1½ teaspoons instead and feed every 2 weeks.

Another good method is to use one of the pelleted slow-release fertilizers. These dissolve slowly over a period of time, releasing nutrients with every watering.

Feed through the growing season if the plant is to receive winter protection. Stop feeding about mid-July if the plant is to remain outdoors. This will give it a chance to harden new growth.

The strawberry plants are planted in a synthetic soil mix (to prevent the spread of verticillum wilt and root rot) in plastic pots sunk in the ground and will produce abundantly. The mulch is shredded fir bark.

Watering Container Plants

Judge when to water by the behavior of your plant. It should never wilt, but neither should it stand in soggy soil. By checking the soil occasionally by digging down an inch or two, you'll learn when and how much to water. The top inch may stay moist for a week in fairly cool weather, but in hot, windy weather you'll need to water more often, perhaps even every day for a plant that needs repotting. (This is why well-drained soil is important: You can water liberally, without drowning the roots.) Don't count on rain to do all of your watering. Plants in containers can act as umbrellas, shedding most of the rainfall. Check the soil even when rain has been abundant.

Vacation watering. When you leave home for a long period of time, group your containers near a water source and away from the afternoon sun. Grouping them will help keep them moist, and the shade will cut the need for water. If they are located near a hose, your vacation waterer won't miss any of them by accident. For large numbers of containers, you can buy water timers that will turn water on at regular intervals. Hook up a system of small hoses to each container. Drip systems are effective too, provided you filter the water before it goes into the system.

Leaching. It is important to leach the soil occasionally to remove built-up mineral salts that can burn plants. Salts build up from fertilizers and from hard water. Any water that won't produce good soapsuds, or which leaves bathtub rings is hard water, and hard water has a high mineral content. Leaching consists of running enough water through the soil to wash away accumulated salts. You'll know you have a salt problem when you see brown leaf edges. Avoid this difficulty by gently hosing the soil in each container for about 20 minutes every 2 months. The water should flow just fast enough to run through the soil and out the drainage holes of the container.

It is also a good idea when watering in hard-water areas to fill the container until water runs freely from the bottom, go on to other containers, then return and repeat the process. This will keep salts to a minimum.

You should also avoid using softened water for watering plants because of the chemicals it contains.

Mulch

Mulch will help keep the soil in your containers moist and cool. Use a coarse organic mulch such as bark chips, and pile it about 2 inches thick.

PLANTING AND CARE

Attention to basic needs assures good fruit and berry crops. Planting is only the first step on the way to a good harvest.

The fruiting plants in this book have been selected because either they produce much finer crops or they tolerate certain conditions better than their wild relatives. But with all of the advances brought to us by plant breeders and growers, good performance of any fruit plant still requires good care on the part of the gardener. In this chapter we discuss how fruit plants produce fruit, how they grow, and what you need to know to get them started and to keep them healthy, beautiful, and productive.

Pollination

You may feel that once you plant a tree you've done your part and the rest is up to nature. This is an idea that easily can lead to fruitless fruit plants. Before you ever lift a shovel—indeed, before you even buy a fruit tree—you need to understand a little about how fruit is produced.

Plant breeding may seem like a subject better suited to the botanist, but every time you bite into an apple or a pear you're tasting the results of plant breeding, particularly of the act of pollination. With a few exceptions (certain figs, for example), fruit will not form unless pollen from the male parts of a flower is transferred to the female parts of a flower. The pollinating insects for most of the fruits in this book are bees. The presence of bees around your plants, however, does not necessarily mean you'll get a crop. The pollen they carry must be of the right sort. Most of us know that apple pollen, for example, will never pollinate a pear blossom; but what is not as commonly known is that apple pollen will not always pollinate an apple blossom.

The Right Combinations

Some plants are called *self-pollinating* or *self-fertile*. This means that their flowers can be fertilized by pollen either from flowers on the same plant, or from another plant of the same kind. Self-fertile plants will produce fruit even if they are planted far away from any other plant of their kind. Among the self-fertile plants are some apples and pears, most peaches and apricots, some plums, all sour cherries, and the entire citrus group.

Other plants set fruit *only* when they receive pollen from a plant of a different cultivar. Their own pollen is ineffective on their own flowers, and they are called *self-sterile*. This group includes many apples, all sweet cherries, and some pears, peaches, apricots, and plums. The 'Napoleon' (or 'Royal Ann') sweet cherry, for example, needs another cherry tree with fertile pollen within 100 feet, or it will bear no fruit. A plant that will fertilize a self-sterile plant is known as a *pollinator*.

Never assume that because you have a bearing fruit tree you can be sure of a crop on a new tree of a different variety planted nearby. Plants must bloom at about the same time for cross-pollination to be successful; so an early self-sterile apple must have another early apple as a pollinator.

Parts of a Flower

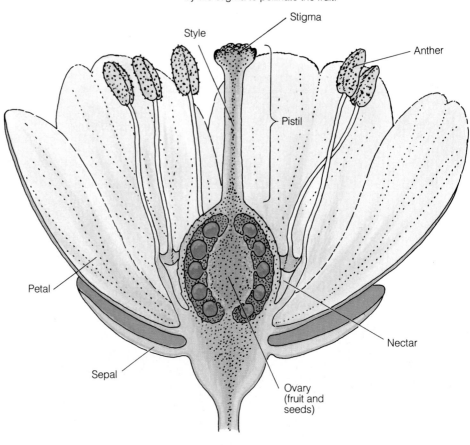

Bees carry pollen on body hair, then brush by the stigma to pollinate the fruit.

Stigma

Style

Anther

Pistil

Petal

Nectar

Sepal

Ovary (fruit and seeds)

Some plants bear male and female flowers on separate plants. Figs and persimmons are among these. Fortunately, most figs and persimmons available to the home gardener will produce fruit without pollination.

Planting for Pollination

A fruit plant that needs a pollinator needs it to be close by. The maximum recommended distance is 100 feet, but the closer the better. This is because bees that carry the pollen are unlikely to fly back and forth if the distance between trees is any greater.

If your neighbor has a pollinating variety across the back fence, you're in good shape; if not, do one of the following:

☐ Plant two different trees fairly close together.
☐ Graft a branch of another variety onto a tree that needs pollination.

Sometimes even though a good pollinator is near the tree that needs it and blooms at the same time, bees will fail to do the job and your crop will be poor. If this occurs, trick the bees by placing a bouquet of flowers from the pollinating tree, in a vase or jar of water, and then lodge the container in the branches of one of the trees. Do this early in the morning when temperatures are relatively low, and the bees are active.

Choosing good pollinators for your plants is a most important part of fruit gardening. The "Encyclopedia of Fruits and Berries," beginning on page 78, will describe which varieties need pollinators and what pollinators you can use when they are necessary.

How to Achieve Proper Pollination

Plant close
to a pollinating
variety.

Hang a bucket of
pollinating blossoms
in a blooming tree.

Graft on a branch of another variety that
will pollinate your tree. Here, two scions
have been inserted in a cleft graft and
protected with grafting wax. Once
established, only the healthier should be
left to mature. The other should be
pruned off.

How Fruit Plants Grow

All plants must have sugar in order to produce energy and grow. They produce sugar through photosynthesis, a process that absorbs sunlight through the leaves and makes sugar from the interaction of carbon dioxide and water. You can stimulate this process and provide plants with more of the sugar they need by: planting them in a sunny spot, pruning and training them for good leaf exposure, keeping the soil properly watered, and keeping leaves free of dust, pests, and disease. Each piece of growing fruit needs about 30 leaves working for it, not including leaves which supply nourishment to roots and branches.

The illustration below gives some idea of the day-to-day workings of a fruit plant. While the leaves are busy topside, roots spread out underground, searching for water, oxygen, and mineral nutrients. These essential elements are then transported to the green tissues of the plant, where photosynthesis is carried out through the energy supplied by sunlight, to manufacture the necessary sugar. The sugar not immediately converted to energy for the plant's survival and growth is stored throughout the plant, including the fruit. It's easy to understand that the greater the supply of factors that produce sugar—sunlight, water, and carbon dioxide—the more abundant and the sweeter the fruit.

Day-to-Day Workings of a Fruit Tree

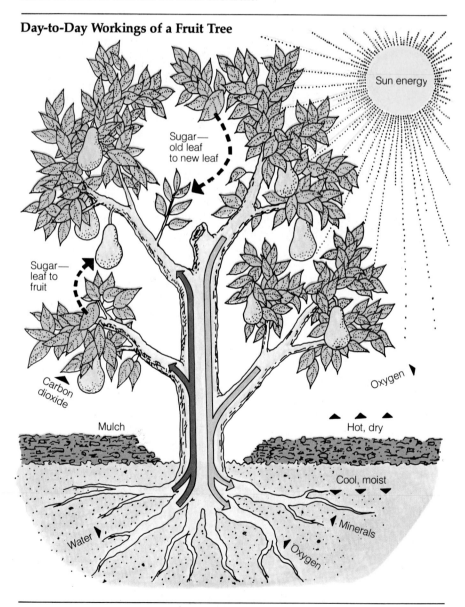

Doctoring

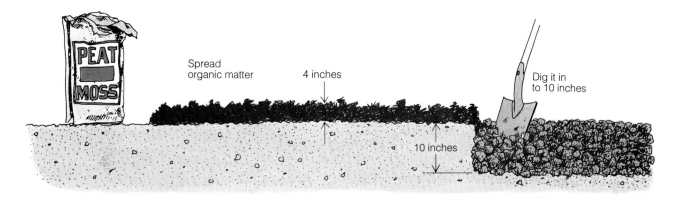

Spread organic matter

4 inches

Dig it in to 10 inches

10 inches

Soil

Soil should provide roots with (1) a good supply of air; (2) constant moisture (but not standing water); and (3) a good supply of mineral nutrients.

You can supply these needs best if you first examine your soil. Is it rock-hard when dry and gummy when wet? If so, you have the very fine-textured soil called *clay*, or *adobe*. Clay holds moisture so well that there is little or no room for air. To correct this, aerate clay soil by adding organic matter such as peat moss or compost. Spread 4 or 5 inches of organic matter over the soil and mix it in evenly. Ideally, you should add organic material to wherever the plant's roots might spread at maturity. Keep in mind that roots spread more widely than the branches.

Does water soak directly into your soil without significant spreading? Does the soil dry up a few days after watering? If so, your soil is likely to be *sandy*. Sandy soils contain a great deal of air, but moisture and nutrients are quickly drained away. Additional organic matter helps here too, by filling in the spaces between the coarse soil particles, and retaining water. Peat moss, compost, and manures are especially beneficial for sandy soils. Sawdust and ground bark are less good at holding water and actually use nutrients as they decay, thus depriving the plant of them.

If you have soil that feels moist for days after watering, but still crumbles easily when you pick up a handful and squeeze it, then it's just right.

Air space is what remains after drainage and water retention of various mixes and their ingredients have been measured. The figures in the chart below indicate percent by volume. The physical properties of clay loam are included in the list for comparison.

Clay is fluffier

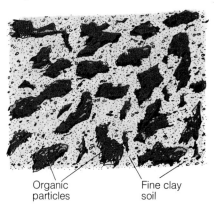

Organic particles

Fine clay soil

Sand holds water

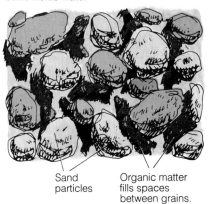

Sand particles

Organic matter fills spaces between grains.

Material	Total Porosity	Water Retention	Air Space After Drainage
Clay loam	59.6	54.9	4.7
Sphagnum peat moss	84.2	58.8	25.4
Fine sand	44.6	38.7	5.9
Redwood sawdust	77.2	49.3	27.9
Perlite, 1/16−3/16"	77.1	47.3	29.8
Vermiculite, 0−3/16"	80.5	53.0	27.5
Fir bark, 0−1/8"	69.5	38.0	31.5
1:1, fine sand; fir bark	54.6	37.4	15.2
1:1, fine sand; peat moss	56.7	47.3	9.4
1:1, perlite, peat moss	74.9	51.3	23.6

Bareroot

Burlap-wrapped

2-gallon
can

Papier-mâché
pot

Some plants tolerate dense, airless, soggy soil better than others. Among the fruits, pears will tolerate dense, wet soil. Apples and crab apples will take short periods of airless soil. Apricots, cherries, figs, nectarines, peaches, plums, grapes, and currants all need fair drainage. Strawberries, cane berries, and citrus need good drainage. Blueberries must have perfect drainage.

Keep in mind that in gardens with extremely dense soil you can still plant fruits that prefer porous soils by using containers or raised beds. A good size for a raised bed to accommodate a standard fruit tree would be 3 feet deep and 6 feet long by 6 feet wide. Soils for containers are discussed on page 35.

Planting

Nurseries and garden centers sell bareroot plants, plants with a rootball wrapped in burlap, and plants growing in containers. Most deciduous fruit plants are sold bareroot.

The leafless bareroot plant is taken from the ground in late fall or winter after it has gone dormant, and shipped to the nursery, where it is held under refrigeration in moist sand or wood shavings. Sometimes the roots are enclosed in a plastic bag full of moist shavings. Bareroot plants are fragile and must be kept cool and moist. Plant them as soon as possible. Bareroot plants are sometimes put into containers at the nursery. If you buy them in winter, or while they're still dormant, you can bare the roots again to plant them. If they have already leafed out, grow them in their containers until May or June, so the root system has time to knit the container soil together.

Evergreen plants are sold with their roots still in soil and wrapped in burlap, or growing in metal or pulp containers. Balled-and-burlapped plants are sold at the same time as bareroot plants and should be quickly put into the ground, or their permanent containers. Those sold in metal containers are available year round and may be held as long as you don't cut the container until time to plant.

Never let bareroot or balled-and-burlapped plants lie unprotected. If you must keep bareroot plants for a time before you are ready to plant, dig a shallow trench, lay the plants on their sides with roots in the trench, and cover the roots with moist soil. This is called "heeling in." Wrap balled-and-burlapped plants in a sheet of plastic so that the soil ball stays moist.

The illustrations on this page will give you some idea of how to plant a tree from the nursery. Remember never to plant if the soil is very wet. Working wet soil packs it down, driving out the air, and trapping the roots. In rainy climates, you can dig holes for the plants in the fall and protect the soil that's removed with a weighted plastic sheet. The soil will then be workable any time.

It's good advice to plant high. Notice in the illustrations that the planting soil is mounded above the normal soil line. The most fragile part of a woody plant is the crown, that section where the soil touches the trunk, and from which the roots branch. The crown must be dry most of the time, especially in spring and fall. Raised planting minimizes crown rot (which can be fatal to the plant) by making it impossible for water to puddle near the trunk. If you plant at soil level, you invite disaster, because the soil in the planting hole will settle, and your plants will sink downward, exposing the crown to moisture.

Be especially careful when planting grafted dwarf fruit trees. Dwarfing rootstocks cause dwarfing because the rootstocks are not vigorous or deep-rooted. Trees on the smallest stocks may become uprooted unless they have support. Many growers now are placing the bud of the fruiting variety high on the rootstock, up to 6 or 8 inches above ground. This bud union shows later as a bulge with a healed scar on one side. Plant the tree with the union about 2 inches above the soil. This is deeper than it grew in the nursery and accomplishes two things: first, the deep planting makes the tree a little more stable; second, the rootstock is less likely to send up suckers from underground. Be careful never to bury the bud union in soil or mulch at any time during the life of the tree. If moist material touches the union, the upper fruiting part will root, and its vigorous root system will produce a full-sized tree, instead of the dwarf you bought. Check the bud union frequently for signs of rooting and keep mulches a few inches away from it.

As a rule of thumb, dig the planting hole twice the width of the rootball. This is a case where it's always better to do more rather than less. A wise gardener once remarked, "It's better to plant a 50-cent tree in a 5-dollar hole than a 5-dollar tree in a 50-cent hole."

Container Planting

Remove can before planting

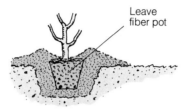
Leave fiber pot

Bareroot Planting

Clip off broken roots. The hole must be wide enough for the roots to spread. Soak the soil after the hole is refilled; make a volcano-shaped mound, then soak again from the top, running water slowly so it sinks in. Mound higher in dense soil, lower in good soil.

Balled-and-Burlapped Planting

Do not jar the rootball or you may damage the tree. After the first layer of fill is pressed down, fold back the burlap and fill again. Soak, make the mound, and soak again. Protect all newly planted trees from winds or strong sun.

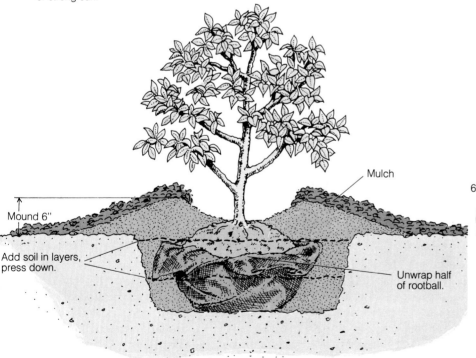

Mulch

Mound 6"

Add soil in layers, press down.

Unwrap half of rootball.

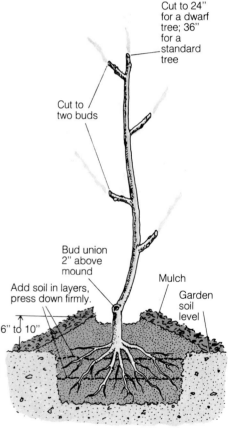

Cut to 24" for a dwarf tree; 36" for a standard tree

Cut to two buds

Bud union 2" above mound

Add soil in layers, press down firmly.

Mulch

Garden soil level

6" to 10"

The symptom of chlorosis is a lack of green color in the leaves. It is frequently caused by an iron deficiency. In many cases the whole leaf turns yellowish except for the veins.

Feeding

When you feed a fruit tree, you are supplying mineral nutrients. The three primary plant nutrients are nitrogen, phosphorus, and potassium. Plants also need three secondary nutrients—calcium, magnesium, and sulfur—and very small quantities of trace nutrients, including iron, manganese, and zinc. Nitrogen in some usable form is the only element that is always in short supply. You can add it in these forms: ammonium nitrate, ammonium sulphate, calcium nitrate, complete fertilizers, or bird or animal manures.

Fruit trees rarely need extra phosphorus, but they will occasionally need potassium and the other nutrients. If growth is slow, or leaves and fruit look unnatural or unhealthy, check with your nursery or agricultural extension agent to find out what should be added.

For a newly planted tree, use a starter solution of a high-phosphorus liquid fertilizer. This will encourage new root growth. Never give nitrogen fertilizer to a newly planted tree. Nitrogen will stimulate leaf growth, which is undesirable until the roots become established. Wait until growth is abundant in late June or early July. Keep all fertilizers away from the area around the trunk of the tree.

Although one or two feedings are often recommended, we suggest feeding equal amounts of chemical fertilizers four times at evenly spaced intervals between early spring and late June. Water very deeply after feeding. Use the following schedules for standard-size trees. Dwarf fruit trees will require proportionately less.

First and second season. 1 tablespoon at each feeding, scattered evenly.

Third to tenth season. Double the amount each year; for example, 2 tablespoons per feeding in the third year, 4 tablespoons in the fourth year, then 8, 16 (one cup), and so on.

Mature tree. Continue feeding with 5 pounds ammonium sulphate; or 3½ pounds ammonium nitrate; or 6 pounds calcium nitrate; or 10 pounds of complete fertilizer containing 10 percent nitrogen.

Feeding with animal manure. Animal manure is lower in nitrogen than chemical fertilizers and it may contain harmful salts. In dry climates be careful of bird and rabbit manures. If leaves show brown edges, soak the root area for several hours and change to another feeding method. Cattle manure is a little safer if you water thoroughly and deeply, and it can act as both food and mulch—but it smells.

Since manures contain less nitrogen per pound than chemical fertilizer, you can use relatively more, but since they release nitrogen slowly through bacterial action, you can also put the whole amount around the tree at one time. For young, growing trees, begin with a little less than ½ pound of bird manure, or about 1 pound of cattle manure, and double each year. For mature trees, use 50 to 70 pounds of well-rotted bird or rabbit manure, spreading it under the outer branches in fall. For the same trees, use 100 to 200 pounds of well-rotted cattle manure.

Feeding is less a matter of exact measurement than it is of how the plant responds. Nitrogen forces leafy growth, but too much can be harmful to your fruit crop. Feed only enough for your tree to grow well. If it produces only a few inches of growth one season, step up feeding. If it sprouts up like a geyser, feed less. And remember, dark leaves mean too much nitrogen; uniformly yellowish leaves mean too little.

Watering

Standard fruit trees need deep watering. Dwarf trees on shallow-rooted stocks may not need as much, but must have a constant moisture supply. At planting time, water each layer of soil in the planting hole. If the garden soil is dry, soak the hole itself before you put in the plant. Finish by soaking from the top of the planting mound, creating a depression to hold the water. Take care that water does not run over the side.

Water thoroughly after planting, and before new growth begins; do not water again unless the soil seems unusually dry. The roots are not growing actively at this time, and soggy soil will invite rot. When new growth begins, let the top inch or so of soil dry; then give the plant a thorough soaking. Be sure to water at the top of the planting mound. This is especially important with burlap-wrapped plants, since the soil in the rootball may not take up water unless it is applied directly overhead.

When first-season growth is abundant, and plants are growing well in midsummer, stop watering from the top of the mound. Dig a shallow ditch at the base, and soak the soil about every 2 to 3 weeks, or whenever the top inch or 2 of soil dries.

After the first season make a shallow ditch about 6 to 12 inches wide around the plant and just outside the tips of the branches. Move the ditch outward as the plant grows (see the illustration below). Soak thoroughly about once every 3 or 4 weeks. This is a rough guide. Your tree may need more water or less, depending on the sandiness of the soil. Always dig down a few inches into the soil first to see if watering is necessary.

Your aim in watering is to soak the soil long enough so that moisture reaches the deep roots. Remember that water sinks quickly through sandy soil, but very slowly through clay. On standard trees the deepest roots may penetrate the soil to a depth of many feet. On dwarf trees the deepest roots

A specialized fertilizer applicator for trees applies nutrients directly to the root zone.

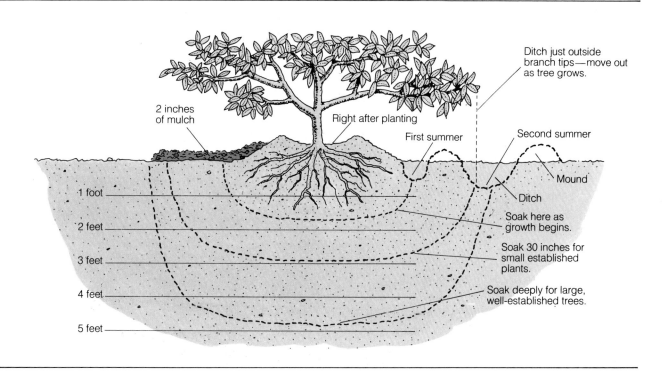

2 inches of mulch

Right after planting

First summer

Second summer

Ditch just outside branch tips—move out as tree grows.

Mound

Ditch

Soak here as growth begins.

Soak 30 inches for small established plants.

Soak deeply for large, well-established trees.

1 foot

2 feet

3 feet

4 feet

5 feet

may extend only to 30 to 36 inches beneath the surface. You can check your watering by pushing a stiff, 4- to 5-foot-long wire into the wet soil. It will penetrate only wet soil, so when it refuses to go down any farther, pull it out and check the depth of penetration. Soil should be moist down to at least 2½ feet for dwarfs, 3½ to 4 feet for standard trees.

Trees in a lawn area should have a deep soaking about twice a summer in addition to normal lawn watering.

Mulching

Mulch is simply a cover over the soil. It may be gravel, sheet plastic, ground fir bark, or any of a number of organic materials. Organic mulches are of particular value because as they break down they improve soil texture and add nutrients. The major advantages of mulch are that it:

☐ Keeps wind and sun from baking and crusting soil.
☐ Smothers weed seeds.
☐ Protects soil from pedestrian traffic.
☐ Holds in water even at the surface.
☐ Keeps surface soil cool (organic mulch) or warm (plastic mulch).
☐ Keeps soil from alternately freezing and thawing, which, in turn, can heave plants from the ground.

The chart on page 49 lists many mulching materials, along with some of their advantages and disadvantages.

Applying mulch. Using a mulch, cover the soil from the planting mound to the branch tips if possible. Use at least 2 inches of a porous material. Slash waterproof mulches like thick paper or plastic at intervals so water can pass

---

Proper Mulching Method

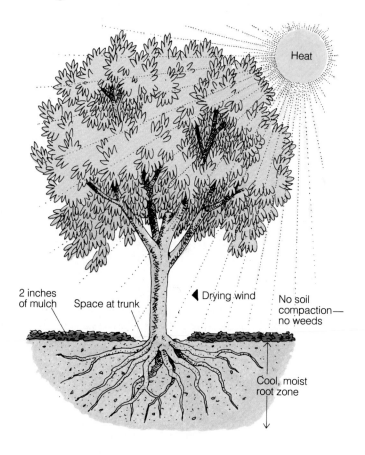

Heat

2 inches of mulch   Space at trunk   ◀ Drying wind   No soil compaction— no weeds

Cool, moist root zone

Mulching Materials

Material	Remarks
Rotted manure	May contain weed seeds.
Sawdust Wood chips Wood shavings	Low in plant nutrients, decomposes slowly, tends to pack down. Well-rotted material preferred. Can be fresh if nitrate of ammonia or nitrate of soda is added at the rate of 1 pound per 100 sq. ft. Keep away from building foundations; may attract termites.
Peat moss	Attractive, available, but expensive for large areas. Should be kept moist at all times.
Ground corn cobs	Excellent for improving soil structure.
Pine needles	Will not mat down. Fairly durable.
Peanut hulls Cotton screenings Tobacco stems (shredded)	Supply plant nutrients and improve soil structure. Fairly durable.
Tree leaves (whole) Tree leaves (shredded)	Excellent source of humus. Rot rapidly, high in nutrients. Oak leaves especially valuable for azaleas, camellias, and rhododendrons.
Hay Grass clippings	Unattractive, but repeated use builds up reserve of available nutrients which lasts for years.
Straw	Same as above, but lower in nutrients although furnishes considerable potassium.
Buckwheat hulls	Very attractive but tend to scatter in windy locations.
Pecan hulls	Extremely durable, availability limited.
Gravel or stone chips	Limited use, but particularly good for rock garden plantings. Extremely durable, holds down weeds, but does not supply plant nutrients or humus.
Bark	Ground and packaged commercially. Especially attractive in this form. Sometimes available in bulk form from pulpwood-loading sites.

through. The appearance of a plastic mulch can be improved with gravel, pebbles, or bark chips spread over the surface about an inch deep. Hide paper mulches with a thin layer of ground bark.

In warm, dry climates, spread organic mulches in spring and turn them into the top 2 inches of soil in late fall. In cold climates where the ground freezes, add more mulch in late fall, up to 6 inches deep. You may even want to cover this deep mulch with evergreen boughs for added protection, and to keep the mulch in place when strong winds blow. Snow will increase the usefulness of any mulch.

Never pile mulch against the tree trunk or plant stem, but keep it at least 6 inches away. Wet mulch can cause rot, and dwarf trees mulched to the bud union will take root and grow to full size. The one exception to the rule is in very cold climates, where it is good to mulch deeply over the bud union when real cold begins. Be sure, however, to remove the mulch when severe cold is over.

Pests and Diseases

The more energy your plants must expend recovering from the effects of pests and diseases, the less fruit they will bear. Here are some tips on giving them a helping hand that will be amply rewarded at harvest time.

Fruit pests. The pests listed here are among the most common, although you may meet others. A few of these are confined to specific regions of the country.

Apple maggot (railroad worm). Primarily a pest east of the Rockies, the apple maggot has adult flies that lay eggs under the skin of the fruit, and larvae that hatch and tunnel through the flesh. The flies are active from July through harvest. Keep trees clean and remove damaged fruit. Spray with diazinon or carbaryl products, following label directions. Do not use diazinon within 14 days of harvest.

Birds. Birds are at their worst with cherries, blueberries, and other fruit they can remove entirely. When fruit begins to ripen, cover the entire plant with a plastic netting, available from nurseries and hardware dealers. Throw the net directly over the plant, or build simple wood frames for

Apple maggot

Birds

Cherry fruit fly

Cherry (pear) slug

Codling moth

Flatheaded borer

Leaf roller

Mites

dwarfs and bushes. For larger fruits, cotton twine may be sufficient discouragement. Throw a ball of it over the tree repeatedly from different sides. The strands annoy the birds when they try to land. The twine will rot away over winter.

Cherry fruit fly. A pest in the Pacific Northwest, the cherry fruit fly starts as a white larva that burrows through the cherries, leaving a hole. As soon as you notice flies or maggot damage, spray at 7-day intervals with diazinon or any product registered for control of this pest. Do not spray diazinon within 14 days of harvest.

Cherry (pear) slug. These small, wet-looking, green worms are the larvae of a wasp. They skeletonize leaves, leaving a lacy patch. Spray when you notice them (probably June, and again in August) with malathion, or a contact spray registered for control of the pest. Follow label directions. Once is usually enough.

Codling moth. The major apple and pear pest, these moths lay eggs in the blossoms, and their larvae tunnel in the fruit, leaving holes and droppings (frass). Spray with diazinon after petals fall and continue at 7 to 10-day intervals as directed.

Flatheaded borer. This western pest burrows into bark that has been damaged and is often found in sunburned trees. To avoid the pest, avoid the damage: Paint or wrap trunks, and be careful not to cut them with tools or machinery. When you find tunnels and droppings, cut away bark and wood and dig out the borers. Be sure you have them all, and then paint the wound with tree seal or asphalt emulsion. For apples, cherries, and pears, use a lindane product registered for control of this pest.

Leaf roller. This moth larva surrounds itself with a rolled leaf and feeds on both foliage and fruit. Once established, it is protected from spray, and must be unrolled by hand. Spray with diazinon when pests first appear and at intervals recommended on the label.

Mites. Spraying for insects may trigger a mite attack, because spraying removes the mites' enemies. You'll know mites are present by a silvery webbing under leaves, or if the leaves curl or bronze. Mites love dry air and dust, so wash off foliage with a jet of water in dusty seasons. Kill overwintering mites with dormant oil spray. During the growing season, use diazinon or malathion products labeled for mite control on fruit trees.

Peach tree borer

Pear psylla

Plum curculio

Rodents

Rosy apple aphid

San Jose Scale

Tent caterpillar

Peach tree borer. There are two kinds of peach borer: One bores into twigs (peach twig borer), and one bores into the trunk at the soil line. The second is very common. Dig soil away from the trunk and check for tunnels and droppings. Kill the worm by pushing a bit of wire down its tunnel. Spray trees with diazinon, carbaryl, or lindane products, according to directions. Check cherry and plum trees for the same pest.

Pear psylla. The youngest stages collect on leaves, like aphids, and suck juices. They drop a honeydew that may cause a fungus growth that coats leaves, blocking photosynthesis, and weakening the tree. Dormant oil spray helps, and early stages can be controlled with carbaryl sprays. Do not use carbaryl during bloom. Malathion also will control psyllids, but do not use within 1 day of harvest.

Plum curculio. Serious on many stone fruits east of the Rockies, this pest belongs to the beetle family, and its larvae attack fruit right after blossom time. Spray with carbaryl or another product labeled for control of this pest and follow directions.

Rodents. Mice, voles, and rabbits all like the bark of young trees, especially when it is covered with mulch or snow in winter, and better food is unavailable. If enough bark is removed, the tree will die at the first growth surge of spring. Protect the lower trunk in winter or year round with a cylinder of hardware cloth. Be sure the cloth doesn't become tight as the tree grows. Check during the season and loosen or replace it.

Rosy apple aphid (and other aphids). Aphids are other leaf-rolling creatures that can damage immature fruit and prevent development. A dormant oil spray kills overwintering eggs, and a contact spray of malathion, carbaryl, or diazinon helps control the insects during the growing season.

San Jose scale. Becoming serious in the West again, this pest is indicated by red spots on fruit, or appears in masses when attacks are serious. They can kill a plant in one or two seasons. Use a delayed dormant oil spray to control mature scales before crawlers hatch or are born. Crawlers can be controlled with malathion or diazinon. Follow all directions.

Tent caterpillar. You probably won't see this pest if you have sprayed early for others. Tent caterpillars build large webs among branches. These webs may contain hundreds of hairy caterpillars that then emerge to eat leaves. Use a product registered for control of tent caterpillars on fruit trees.

Apple scab

Bacterial leaf spot

Bacterial gummosis

Brown rot

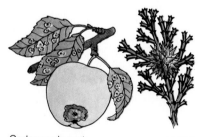

Cedar apple rust

Diseases of fruit trees. The following are the most common of the many fruit tree diseases. Some are easily controlled with proper sprays (using them in the right season is very important); others are best fought by choosing disease-resistant varieties; and some require removal and burning of infected parts.

Any disease is easier to deal with if fruit trees are kept well pruned, and the ground around them clean of fallen fruit and leaves. Pick shriveled fruit that hangs on and either burn it, or seal it in a bag to be discarded.

Be sure to prepare soil properly, plant high, and keep the tree watered and fed. A healthy plant is much more resistant to disease.

Apple scab. This disease lives between growing seasons on fallen leaves, so adequate garden cleanup is important. The fungus produces two kinds of spores: one in spring, another in summer. Both attack foliage and fruit, growing whenever it rains. The disease is no problem in dry-summer climates. Both apples and crab apples are affected and need sprays. Choose resistant plants when possible.

To control scab, apply a recommended fungicide to apples at regular intervals, as directed. The manufacturer's label will include a schedule for optimum results.

Bacterial leaf spot. Primarily attacking cherries and plums, this disease lives over in old leaves, and produces spores in spring. The spores begin infections during rainy periods, causing colored spots that turn brown and cause widening holes on the leaves. It may attack fruit spurs and cause fruit drop.

To control, spray with a recommended fungicide at petal fall, covering the leaves thoroughly. Spray as directed on the product label.

Bacterial gummosis. Deposits of gum along stone fruit branches is fairly common and may occur because of mechanical damage, insect damage, or as a result of a number of diseases. Several serious bacterial diseases with this symptom almost rule out the planting of certain fruit varieties in some areas. There is no spray treatment. Two diseases that often cause gumming are:

☐ *Bacterial canker of cherries.* In wet climates avoid 'Bing', 'Lambert', 'Napoleon', and 'Van' cultivars. Resistant cultivars are 'Corum' and 'Sam'. The disease causes long, narrow, damp-looking, gum-edged patches on trunk or branches. Branches die as they are girdled. The disease can affect apricots, blueberries, peaches, and prune plums. Choose resistant peaches from the cultivars list.

☐ *Coryneum blight of peaches.* This is a fungus disease primarily of peaches, but also of cherries, apricots, and prune plums. Spotty leaves and fruit are followed by darkened bark that ruptures and exudes gum. It is controllable. Use fixed copper in October, then in spring before new buds open. In milder climates use wettable sulfur as a spray 1 week after petal fall and again after rainy periods.

Brown rot. This disease is serious on all stone fruits, but especially on nectarines in some regions, making them nearly impossible to grow to the edible stage. The disease first causes blossoms to brown and turn wet-looking, then drop. The amount of blossom blight indicates the amount of fruit that may be spoiled. Brown rot eventually makes fruit shrivel and dry on the tree. It must be removed by hand to prevent reinfection.

To control the blossom-blight phase, spray as the first pink shows, using a fungicide such as Benlate, captan, Cyprex, ferbam, ziram, or lime sulfur. Spray as directed on the product label.

To control attacks on fruit, spray as the fruit begins to ripen (green fruit is rarely attacked) and repeat if there is a period of wet weather. On peaches and nectarines, the disease may attack twigs and live over within them. Pruning out any dead twigs helps control the disease in the following year.

Cedar apple rust. This disease appears only where the alternate host, red cedar, grows near apples. The leaves first show orange spots and odd, cup-shaped structures; then they yellow and fall. Remove red cedars, or avoid planting them. If you have ornamental cedars, remove the galls in summer. They are brownish and globe-shaped, and look like part of the tree. Spray the apples with a product registered for control of cedar apple rust (ferbam or zineb products), following directions carefully.

Crown gall. This disease of bacterial origin occurs in some soils. It attacks young trees, producing soft galls or swellings on the crown and roots. The galls grow until they girdle and kill the tree. There is no chemical control.

Crown gall

Avoid buying young trees that show galls, and plant young trees carefully to avoid injury, as injury allows bacteria to enter the plant. Older trees with galls can only be removed and destroyed. Recent experimental work has indicated that young plants can be inoculated against the disease, but no immunization is yet available.

Crown rot. This is a common serious disease of almost any plant so planted that the trunk is constantly wet at the soil line during spring and fall. Crown rot is caused by a fungus, and appears late in the growing season. Infected branches redden, and foliage yellows or discolors.

Look at the bark below the soil line to see whether it is dead. If it is, scrape the bark away and pull back soil so that air can reach the infection. Avoid crown rot on established trees by planting high and watering well out from the trunk. The soil should never be wet at the crown.

Fireblight

Fireblight. Fireblight is spread by insects during the bloom period and shows later in spring as new growth wilts, turns dark, and finally blackens as if burned. The infection spreads quickly down branches, eventually killing infected pears, and damaging or killing apples.

No treatment has proven completely effective for the home gardener, other than severe pruning and burning of infected wood. Choose resistant pears. For apples, where the disease is severe, plant such resistant cultivars as 'Cortland' or 'Delicious'. Mild winters will increase the severity of the disease the following spring.

To control infection on resistant plants, cut any blighted branches several inches below the infection as soon as you notice an attack. There is some question about how best to sterilize pruning tools, but the classic method is to carry a strong solution of household bleach with you and dip the shears after each cut. Burn all prunings immediately.

Peach leaf curl

Peach leaf curl. This disease is easy to control, but is sure to attack peaches in many regions. Uncontrolled, it will weaken trees, killing them after a number of seasons. It interferes with blossom and fruit production.

To control curl, you must spray any time after leaf fall during dormancy, with a fixed copper spray or lime sulfur, wetting every twig and branch completely. If rain falls immediately after treatment, repeat the treatment.

The disease shows as a reddening of leaves; they then curl into blisters, which may have a powdery look, and finally they fall. A second crop of leaves grows, which is not affected. No spraying is effective once the disease has appeared, but a copper spray or lime sulfur will control it completely if you spray every year.

Powdery mildew. Powdery mildew is a fungus that causes a grayish, powdery coating to form over young shoots, leaves, and flower buds, possibly deforming or killing them. It thrives in shade, and where air circulation is poor. Be sure that fruit plants receive sunlight most of the day and grow where air moves freely. Occasionally rinse dust and mildew spores from the foliage with a strong spray from the hose during the spring and summer.

Powdery mildew

Where an infection begins, clip off severely mildewed twigs and spray the tree with Actidione PM, karathane, or wettable sulfur. Sulfur should not be used during the hottest part of the day.

Spraying fruit trees at proper intervals controls pests and diseases.

Basic Fruit-Pest Control

Complete control of insects and diseases on fruit crops requires a thorough and comprehensive spray program. Proper timing, good coverage of foliage, and correct chemicals are essential.

Here is a simplified spray program that should meet your essential needs. But keep in mind that some pests are difficult to control, so you may find blemished fruit even after following these recommendations. Your neighbors' spray programs are important too. If neighbors are negligent, you may find their problems have become yours.

Apples and pears

Winter. Before leaves are out, apply a dormant oil spray to control scale, mites, and other pests. This can be the most important spray of the year. Follow directions fully and completely for best results.

Spring. The next important spray is when fruit buds show pink at the tips. Spray with an insecticide such as diazinon to control aphids, leaf rollers, and many other pests, and with a fungicide such as captan to control apple scab, fruit spot, and bitter rot. When three-fourths of the petals have fallen, spray an insecticide again to stop codling moth, which appears at this time. Where apple scab is a problem, consistent use of a fungicide such as captan is necessary for control.

Summer. The first summer spray is 10 to 14 days after petal fall. Use an insecticide, fungicide, or both, as your trees require. For perfect fruit, continue to spray through the summer with insecticide and fungicide, as needed.

Fall. Spray as necessary, but pay strict attention to label instructions regarding time intervals between sprays and harvest.

Peaches, apricots, cherries, and plums

Winter. Same as for apples and pears. Where peach leaf curl is a problem, timing is very important. Lime sulfur sprays such as 26 percent calcium polysulfides should be applied in October or November after leaf drop. In winter rainfall areas, do this before heavy rains begin. Apply another full-coverage spray in early spring before buds begin to swell. Note: If buds have begun to swell or open, it is too late to obtain satisfactory control, as infection has already occurred. For best results, apply sprays in fall and early spring.

Spring. When blossom buds show color—pink for peaches, red for apricots, popcorn stage for cherries, and green-tip stage for plums—spray an insecticide such as diazinon to control insect pests. A fungicide such as captan is often needed to control brown rot. Spray an insecticide and fungicide again when three-fourths of the petals have fallen.

Summer. Same as for apples and pears.

Fall. Same as for apples and pears.

PRUNING AND TRAINING

The main objective in pruning is to admit light and air to the interior leaves and fruit. Training allows for cultivation in limited spaces.

This chapter deals with two operations of great importance to the gardener who grows fruits: pruning and training. We first give you the basics of pruning fruit plants, then show how they apply to training plants into functional shapes, and finally look at techniques for training them into more formal shapes. Keep in mind there is no clear division between these operations—most training is pruning.

Pruning

Is it really necessary for the home gardener to learn how to prune? Most of us have seen long-neglected apple or pear trees, or tangles of blackberry vines that may never have seen the pruning shears yet which still bear delicious fruit.

Plants will live, grow, and bear fruit without ever being pruned. Experience has shown, however, that in some plants many problems can arise that are easily prevented or remedied with good pruning. Pruning is probably best viewed as the most effective means to head off trouble and, better yet, to improve your plants' performance and keep them in excellent condition.

Pruning means simply removing part of a plant to benefit the whole. When you cut away any part of a plant—a branch or even a twig—it directly affects the plant's growth. Depending upon how and when it is done, pruning can:

☐ Produce new growth where it is desired.
☐ Help control growth.
☐ Help control size.
☐ Shape a young plant.
☐ Correct or repair damage.
☐ Help control insects and diseases.
☐ Rejuvenate or reshape an older plant.
☐ Bring about earlier blooming.
☐ Increase the production, size, and quality of fruit.

These advantages make pruning well worth undertaking, even if you are inexperienced and, like many, timid about cutting your plants.

Good pruning requires knowledge, foresight, and care. As a rule of thumb, never make a cut without a clear idea of its probable effect on the plant. At the same time, however, don't be so fearful of cutting that you can't get the job done. If you keep in mind that proper pruning is beneficial to plants, and proceed carefully, you'll get good results.

Getting started. No job can be done well without the right tools. To start, you'll need a good pair of pruning shears, and if you plan to be making cuts larger than shears can handle, you'll need more tools, as shown in the illustration on page 58. It's worth noting that the best-quality pruning tools

Getting Started

Illustrated here are the main pruning tools. You should buy: (1) quality shears; (2) a lopper for larger branches; (3) a saw for very large cuts (saws may be folding, straight, or with replaceable blades); (4) a large rasp; (5) a pole saw and a pole pruner. Have shears and loppers sharpened every year, and never force them through too large a branch. You will also need pruning compound and pruning paint to protect fresh cuts.

You may find a large rasp handy for evening up rough edges and smoothing off shoulders. You can rent or buy a pole saw and pole pruner for cutting high branches without climbing.

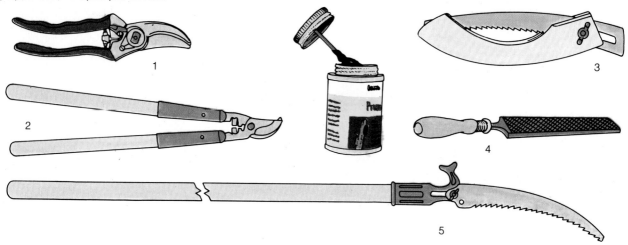

are generally more expensive but are worth the extra cost in the long run, as they will last many years longer than inexpensive tools.

If, at the beginning, you find yourself in a quandary as to where to begin, remember that you can't hurt a plant by cutting out dead, diseased, or damaged wood, or wood that crosses and rubs against other wood (which can cause wounds susceptible to infection). On the contrary, you'll be doing the plant a service. Eliminating these problems is the place to start for the inexperienced and experienced pruner alike. It will provide a clearer view of the tree and of the remaining work to be done, and will also start opening up the tree to more air and light.

Plants vary in their needs for pruning. Some need a good deal every year for maximum health; some need only a little in an entire lifetime; and some never need pruning unless injured. No other plants in the garden are so dependent on pruning as fruit trees. Unfortunately, no other trees vary as widely in the most effective means of pruning.

The objective in pruning a fruit tree is to produce an abundance of good-quality fruit throughout the branches, including the lower and interior ones. An unpruned tree will bear fruit mostly on branch tips. This is because it is the leaves that produce the sugars that, in turn, nourish the plant and accumulate in the fruit. Leaves will grow only where they receive sufficient light. An unpruned tree will have unnecessary growth in its interior, which will cut off some light to the interior, and also restrict air circulation. Lack of air circulation makes the tree more vulnerable to fungus diseases. In addition, heavy loads of fruit at branch tips can make harvesting difficult, and, worse, result in splitting and breaking branches, again causing wounds susceptible to pests and disease.

To head off these problems and produce an even distribution of leaves and fruit, you need to thin out the tree by removing selected branches. The increased light and air circulation achieved by such pruning will help prevent fungus diseases that flourish in poor circulation; open the tree and facilitate spraying; allow the tree to bear more uniformly; and make harvesting easier. Clearly, then, the main objective in fruit tree pruning is to cut to admit light and air to interior leaves and fruit.

The illustrations on page 59 will help you recognize the various parts of a plant you should know when you set to work.

Buds

Look at a dormant plant in winter and you will see rows of buds on the branches, more numerous on small twigs than on old wood. Since the last bud on a branch tends to grow best, you can direct growth by finding a bud that points toward the area where you want a branch and cutting just above it.

Terminal bud. The fat bud at a branch tip will always grow first and fastest if you leave it. Cut it, and several buds will grow behind it.

Leaf bud. Flat triangle on the side of a branch. To make one grow, cut just above it. Choose buds pointing outward from the trunk so the growing branch will have space and light.

Flower bud. Plump compared to leaf buds and first to swell in spring. On stone fruits they grow alone or beside leaf buds. On apples and pears they grow *with* a few leaves.

Spurs. Twiglets on apples, pears, plums, and apricots. They grow on older branches, produce fat flower buds, then fruit. Don't remove them.

Bud scar: A ring on a branch that marks the point where the terminal bud began growing after the dormant season. The line marks the origin of this year's growth.

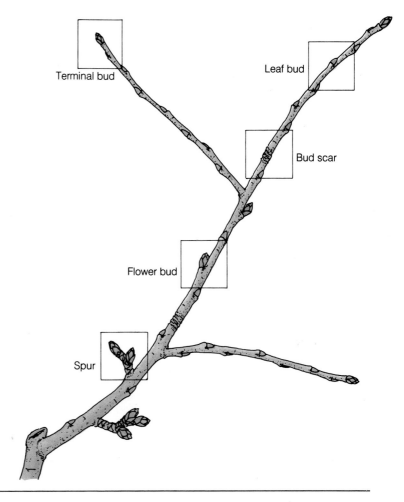

Terminal bud

Leaf bud

Bud scar

Flower bud

Spur

Node

On a leafy branch, a node is the point where stems are attached. Pull off a leaf with its stem, and just above the scar you can see a young bud hidden in the *axil*. Growth enzymes are concentrated there.

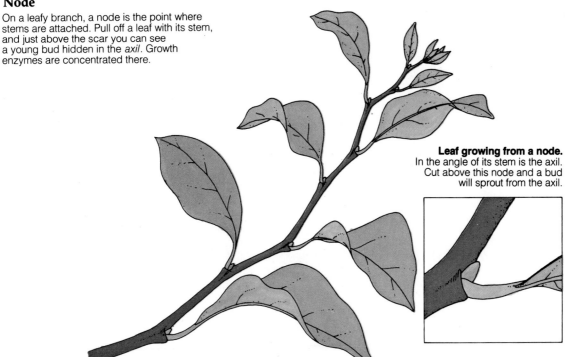

Leaf growing from a node.
In the angle of its stem is the axil.
Cut above this node and a bud
will sprout from the axil.

Making a cut. When you cut away part of a plant, you leave a wound susceptible to pests or disease. To avoid trouble, always try to make wounds as small as possible. If they are over ½ inch in diameter, it's a good idea to protect them with pruning paint, or commercial pruning sealer.

The smallest possible wound is made by removing a bud or twig. If a new sprout is growing in toward the center of the tree or toward the trunk, or threatens to tangle with another branch when it grows longer, pinch it off now, to save pruning later. If you see the bud of a sucker down near the soil, rub it off with your thumb.

Always make cuts close to a node. Branches grow only at these nodes, and if you leave too long a stub beyond the node, it will die and rot. Be sure to cut at a slight angle so that there is no straight "shoulder" left to attract disease or burrowing pests.

The illustrations on this page show you how to make pruning cuts that will heal well.

Making a Cut

When you cut away parts of a plant, you leave a wound where pests or disease organisms can enter. To avoid trouble, try to make wounds as small as possible, and protect them until they heal if they are over a half inch in diameter.

The smallest possible wound is made when you remove a bud or twig. If a new sprout grows in toward the trunk, or threatens to tangle with another branch when it's longer, pinch it off right away and save pruning later. If you see the bud of a sucker down near the soil, rub it off with your thumb.

Make your cuts close to a node. The branches grow only at these nodes, and if you cut between them, the stub will die and rot. Cut at a slight angle so no straight shoulder is left to attract disease or burrowing pests.

Do major pruning in early spring, just as the buds swell. New growth will begin to heal the cuts immediately.

Angle your cut. Cut at an angle about ¼ inch above a bud or leaf. As the bud grows, new bark will cover the raw wood.

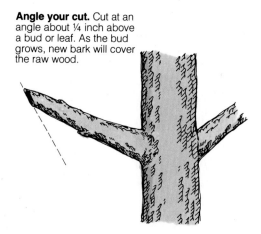

Removing a stub. Never leave a projecting stub. It will rot and can damage the branch it is attached to. Cut stubs close to the trunk at a point where the wound will be about the same diameter as the branch you cut. Cutting *very* close leaves a larger wound.

Cutting a big limb. When you remove a big branch, first undercut at a short distance from the trunk (A). Then saw off the branch beyond the undercut (B). Finally, cut the stub close to the trunk (C). This technique will prevent a falling branch from tearing the bark. Paint the wound with a pruning compound.

Right

Wrong

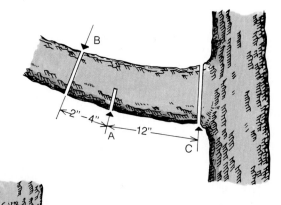

A well-healed cut. New tissue grows from the edge of a wound toward the center. If your cut was smooth, the scar will close evenly with a dimple in the center.

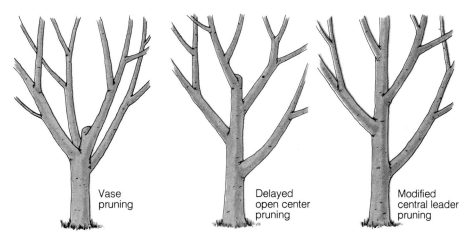

Vase
pruning

Delayed
open center
pruning

Modified
central leader
pruning

Pruning Methods

During the first three years of cultivation, most fruit trees can be pruned in the same way. When they begin to bear, however, each species should be pruned differently. All bearing fruit trees can be pruned annually, with additional light pruning in the summer to expose fruit spurs.

Commercial fruit growers prune fruit trees in three ways, and each has its own advantages. Some growers use the older method called "vase pruning." An alternative and more popular method is "modified central-leader pruning." The third method, "delayed open-center pruning," combines both techniques. Remember that dwarf trees will require less severe pruning because they are smaller.

Vase pruning. The tree is shaped to a short trunk of about 3 feet, with 3 or 4 main limbs, each of which has fully filled-out secondary branches. This shape produces an open center, allowing light to reach all branches.

Vase pruning is always used with apricots, plums, and peaches, and often with pears and apples.

Modified central-leader pruning. The tree is shaped to one tall trunk that extends upward through the tree, clearly emerging at the top. This shape makes a strong tree, but as the center is shaded, less fruit is produced. The smallest dwarf apples are pruned in this shape in a variation called the "spindle bush." Because the tree is as small as a bush, shade and pruning are not problems.

Delayed open-center pruning. This method produces both the strength of a central trunk and the sun-filled center of a vase-shaped tree. A single trunk is allowed to grow vertically until it reaches 6 to 10 feet tall. It is then cut off just above a branch. Main scaffold branches are then selected and pruned to form a vase shape. Subsequent prunings follow the vase method.

A productive fruit tree requires that a definite method of pruning be established from the moment the tree is planted. Such pruning and training will keep the tree balanced in form and—very important—balanced in new and young wood. Left unpruned, the tree will become dense with weak, twiggy growth, and overloaded with small, less healthy fruit.

The Method of Vase Pruning

Since this method of pruning is most frequently used, the general requirements for establishing a vase shape are given. Be sure to consult the specific procedures for each kind of fruit tree given on pages 63–66.

When you plant a young bareroot tree it will normally consist of only a thin vertical shoot, called a *whip*, and some twiggy side branches. To start the tree on a good course, cut the whip back to about 2 feet above the ground for a dwarf, 3 feet for a standard tree. Cut just above a bud, and then prune any side branches back to two buds.

Scaffold. The main limbs branch from the trunk. They should be widely spaced up and down the trunk or a weak, cup-shaped crotch will form and then split when the tree reaches full size.

Vase pruning

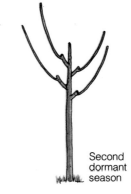

First dormant season

Second dormant season

Third dormant season

Crotch. A crotch is the angle where branches fork, or where a main limb joins the trunk. Strong crotches are wide angled—45 degrees or more. Weak crotches are narrow. As branches enlarge, weak crotches are pinched in the narrow angle and split apart easily.

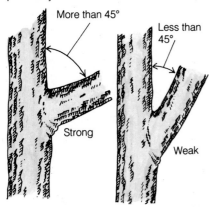

More than 45°

Less than 45°

Strong

Weak

When you plant. Cut off the central stem or whip at 24 to 36 inches above the ground. Use the shorter length for a dwarf, the longer for a standard tree. Cut just above a bud. Stake freestanding dwarf trees on the windward side at planting time and tie loosely. Clip side branches to two buds.

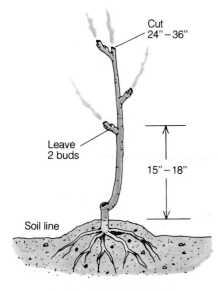

Cut 24"–36"

Leave 2 buds

15"–18"

Soil line

First dormant season. After the new tree has grown through the first spring, summer, and fall, and into its first winter dormancy, choose three or four branches with wide crotches, as shown in the illustration.

Examining the tree from above, look for branches that radiate around the trunk with almost equal distance between them. You should also try to have at least 6 inches vertical distance between branches, with the lowest branch about 18 inches above the ground. If there are three such branches, cut off the vertical stem just above the top one. If there are fewer than three good branches, leave the vertical stem and choose the remaining scaffold branches during the next dormant season.

Second dormant season. If still necessary, choose remaining scaffold branches, and cut off the vertical stem just above the highest selected scaffold branch. The scaffold branches you chose during the first dormant season will have grown side branches. Remove the weakest of these, leaving the main stem and laterals on each branch. *Do not prune twiggy growth.*

Third dormant season. Now is the time to thin surplus shoots and branches. Select the strongest and best-placed terminal shoot near the tip of each scaffold branch, as well as one or two other side shoots on each branch. Remove all other shoots on the branch. Leave the short weak shoots that grow straight from the trunk to shade it and help produce food for the tree.

Mature trees. After the third season in the ground, a fruit tree will need only light thinning until it begins to bear. About a month before the fruit is to be picked, *summer pruning* can be done to expose the fruit to more light and air (see page 76). Shorten new shoots to 3 or 4 inches, wherever this will bring sunlight to the fruit.

It is always necessary to *thin the fruit* if you want large-size, top-quality fruit for home use. Otherwise, nature will produce the most fruit in order to get the largest number of seeds to perpetuate the species. Cherries are the only exception to this rule and are rarely, if ever, thinned.

Although each variety has a best time for thinning, a general guide is to thin before the fruit has gone through half its growing season. Thin an early variety, therefore, much earlier in the summer than later types. Apricots should be thinned to about 2 to 4 inches between fruit, and peaches, nectarines, and the larger plums to about 4 or 5 inches. For the biggest apples, leave about 6 to 8 inches of space, and no more than one apple per fruit spur. The tree has only so much food and energy, and you have a choice of one large apple or two or more small ones.

If you want to see how much difference thinning makes, leave a branch unthinned and compare its fruit at harvest time to that of a properly pruned branch.

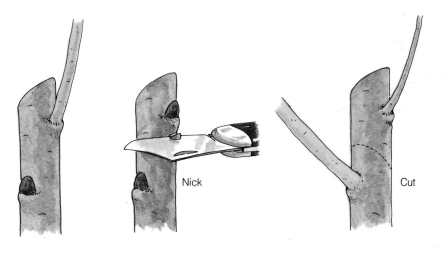

Nick   Cut

The New Apple Tree

You can start the vase method with apple trees as follows: After heading back, the bud immediately below the cut always emerges at too narrow an angle and will eventually develop into a new central leader. A scaffold branch trained from a narrow-angled bud will be weak. To correct this problem, nick the stem just below the bud. Nutrients will be diverted to the bud below, which will grow at a wider, stronger angle. The following dormant season, cut the weakened top bud off.

Pruning Procedures

Apple trees. Vase pruning has been the method commonly used by orchardists to train standard trees. After you have picked your 3 or 4 scaffold branches, as described earlier, cut them back one-third to encourage a strong branch system near the trunk. In the second and third dormant season, reduce the length of all new growth by one-third, and thin out to create a strong, evenly spaced framework of branches. These secondary scaffold branches are the ones that will develop fruit spurs on their lateral branches. The pruning during this period should always be to a bud on the top of a branch pointing outwards, causing the vase shape to develop.

The modified central-leader system is not recommended for a standard tree.

With semidwarf and dwarf apple trees, open head, or vase pruning can be used, but other systems give better and faster results. The modified central-leader system makes these trees stronger and earlier bearing. When planting the bareroot dwarfs, cut back all branches, including the top, about one-fourth, or about 8 to 10 inches. Make cuts to a strong outside bud. For second and third year, repeat the process to train the central leader up and the scaffold branches out, parallel to the ground. Most dwarfs will begin to bear the second and third years, and bear heavily thereafter. For dwarf apples or Malling 9 rootstock, spindle-bush training is also effective.

The Spindle Apple Bush

When you plant. Cut the whip of your Malling 9 dwarf at 20 inches above ground. Trim branches to two buds. Place a 6 foot stake on the windward side and tie the tree loosely.

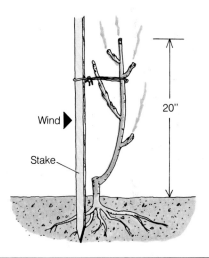

Wind ▶

Stake

20"

Modified central leader pruning

First dormant season. Choose three or four branches evenly spaced around the trunk, and all growing at about the *same* height above the ground. If a crotch is narrow, tie a weight to the branch to pull it outward.

Remove any side branches on the next 18 inches of trunk. Do not cut the vertical stem.

Second dormant season. Choose a second circle of branches growing close together about 20 to 24 inches above the first circle. Leave three or four, evenly spaced around the trunk. Cut side branches above these, but not the vertical stem.

Trim off the weakest side shoots on the lower circle, leaving the best ones and any twiggy growth. Retie the tree loosely.

Third dormant season. Cut all growth along the central stem for about 20 inches above the second circle of branches. In succeeding years, prune to maintain a triple tier, but remove as little growth as possible.

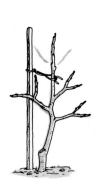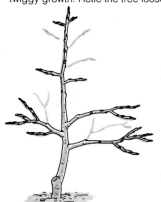

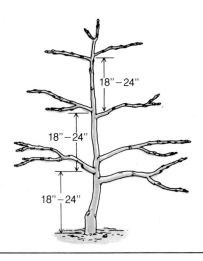

18"–24"

18"–24"

18"–24"

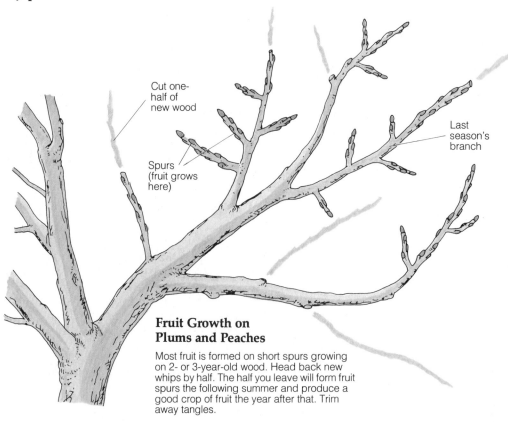

Cut one-
half of
new wood

Spurs
(fruit grows
here)

Last
season's
branch

**Fruit Growth on
Plums and Peaches**

Most fruit is formed on short spurs growing
on 2- or 3-year-old wood. Head back new
whips by half. The half you leave will form fruit
spurs the following summer and produce a
good crop of fruit the year after that. Trim
away tangles.

Pruning a Young Sweet Cherry

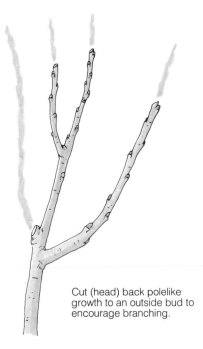

Cut (head) back polelike
growth to an outside bud to
encourage branching.

Apricot trees. Apricots appear on the previous season's shoots, but the bulk of the fruit appears on 4-year-old spurs on older wood, and the spurs drop soon after. To encourage spurs, pinch the lateral shoots when they are about 3 inches long.

Heavy pruning is essential to apricot production. Without it, apricots will start fruiting with heavy crops, but the crops will dwindle as lush foliage shades the lower fruit spurs. Fruit will then be borne only high in the tree.

Plan to shape the young apricot to a wide-spreading head, and keep it low. To maintain this shape, a tree will have to be severely thinned and headed annually. A good apricot tree has a stubby look, and no long, thin branches. The rule is to remove a third of the new wood each year both by thinning and heading. Do this in the winter when the tree is dormant.

When the fruit spurs on a branch are three years old—you can tell by counting the annual bud scar rings—select a new lateral branch, and remove the old one after the fourth season. The fruit will then appear mainly on the new branch. Remove a third of the older lateral branches each year.

Cherry trees. As the sweet cherry grows it should be pruned to the modified central-leader system, as described earlier. Make sure that the leader, or upper scaffold branches, are not choked by lower scaffold branches growing upward. After the tree begins to bear, prune out only weak branches, those that develop at odd angles, or those that cross other branches. Be sure to head back the leader and upright side branches to no more than 12 to 15 feet, so that the mature tree can be kept at about 20 feet.

Sour cherry trees differ from sweet cherries in that they tend to spread wider and are considerably smaller. In fact, some varieties resemble large bushes. The sour cherry can be pruned as a modified central-leader, or—if you prefer to keep the tree smaller—the vase shape. It is quite easy to keep the sour cherry under 12 feet with either system.

Fig trees. Because fig trees bear fruit on wood 1 year old or older, pruning is necessary only to shape a tree for its health and convenient picking. Prune figs to suit the growing situation. Different varieties grow in different ways. The 'California Black' and the 'Adriatic' grow like a spreading shrub. Do not head these trees back, for they will never grow tall or wide. Select scaffold branches at the first dormant period and prune to keep future branches off the ground. Each year, remove low branches that touch the ground or interfere with picking.

The 'Kadota' fig is a vigorous grower that should be kept low-headed and spreading. Head new growth short in the middle of a tree and longer on the outside. When a tree reaches its mature shape, head new growth back 1 or 2 feet.

Peach trees. Most newly planted young peach trees are pruned to the vase or open form. When the tree is planted, cut it off at between 24 and 30 inches in height and leave 3 or 4 laterals to grow into the vase form. These should be headed back the second year only, and only if they exceed 28 or 30 inches in length. These laterals should be spaced evenly around the trunk and 6 to 8 inches apart vertically.

After the second year, peach trees should be pruned lightly. Heavy pruning will result in a weak tree. During the second and later years, the object is to prune for an open center, or bowl-shaped tree. This requires that all branches other than the main three or four be removed from the trunk, and the vertical rising shoots on the remainder be pruned off. Your ultimate goal is to have a wide tree with an open top, 12 to 13 feet high. As the tree grows, cut the upward growing foliage back to outward-growing laterals.

When the tree reaches 10 or 12 feet and is maturing, start severely cutting back the new growth on the top of the tree, being sure to maintain the open center that will admit light to the lower inside parts of the tree. In general, pruning should be lighter on young, bearing trees, than on older peach trees.

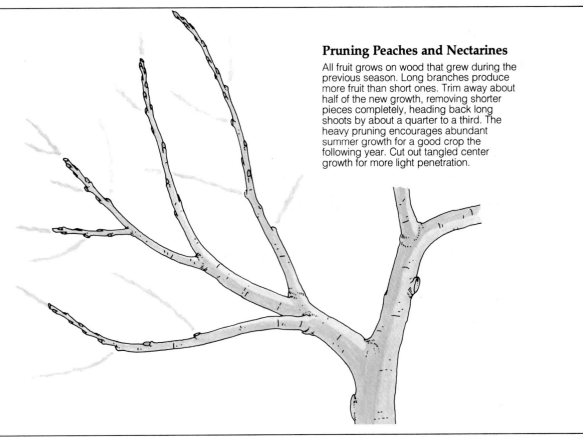

Pruning Peaches and Nectarines

All fruit grows on wood that grew during the previous season. Long branches produce more fruit than short ones. Trim away about half of the new growth, removing shorter pieces completely, heading back long shoots by about a quarter to a third. The heavy pruning encourages abundant summer growth for a good crop the following year. Cut out tangled center growth for more light penetration.

Pear trees. You should train the young pear tree to the modified central-leader system by selecting 5 or 6 scaffold branches over a two-year period. Since it is characteristic of pear varieties to grow upright, be careful not to have too many heading-back cuts, for they will promote too many upright shoots. If you want a small pear tree, buy a dwarf; don't try to make a standard smaller by heavy pruning.

The pear is very susceptible to fireblight, especially in the soft succulent growth that results from heavy pruning, so be careful about heading back or thinning shoots on mature trees. Once fireblight takes hold, there is very little that can be done, except to remove infected growth.

Plum trees. Prune all plums in the winter when dormant. Plums fruit on wood produced the previous year and on spurs on older branches. They are particularly prone to branch splitting when mature and bearing heavy crops.

There are many plum varieties, but they fall into two groups: the European and the Japanese. European plums include prune trees, which bear a fruit whose high percentage of sugar allows it to dry without fermentation. Prunes are left on the tree until they fall or are shaken loose.

The main distinction between European and Japanese plums is the length of the fruiting spurs. The European spurs may reach 3 feet long, much longer than the 3-inch spur of Japanese types. Since the fruit buds are so spread out, far less thinning is needed, and the long, bushlike mass of spurs does not require the severe pruning given Japanese varieties.

Japanese varieties include most of the dessert plums found at the market, the 'Santa Rosa' and 'Satsuma', for example. Some trees grow upright and some spread out, but all fruit in this group is borne on stubby spurs no longer than 3 inches. These spurs will bear for from 6 to 8 years.

Remove one-third of the new wood each year by thinning and heading. This heavy pruning is necessary to produce larger fruit. Keep long, thin branches headed to shape a tree into stubby, wide form. When the fruit spurs on a branch have borne for 6 or 8 years, select a new branch from lateral shoots on this branch. The next year, remove most of the old branch, cutting it off just above the selected lateral.

Remember that any heavily pruned tree sends out abundant new growth in the spring. If a tree bears on older wood, heavy pruning will cut back fruit production. If it bears on new wood, heavy pruning will stimulate production in the season after the following winter.

Pruning always removes some fruiting wood, but an unpruned tree may bear too heavily, and produce small fruit and next to no new growth. Proper pruning produces even crops over many seasons.

New and Old Wood

New wood is the portion of each branch that grew most recently. In winter, during dormancy, you can distinguish new wood by its smoother, paler bark and lack of side growth. Old wood is darker, rougher, and twiggier.

Old

New

Twig

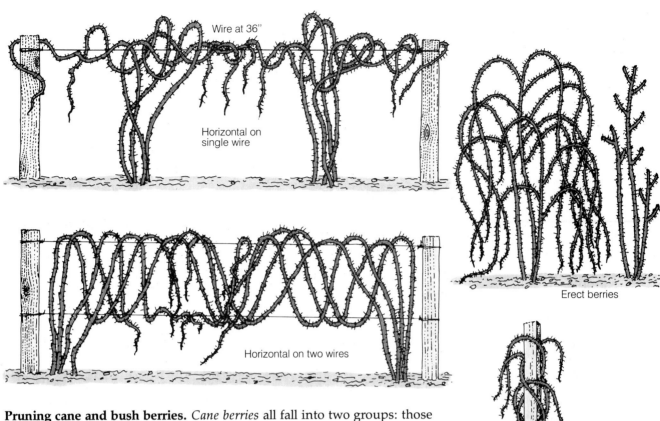

Wire at 36"

Horizontal on
single wire

Horizontal on two wires

Erect berries

Vertical on post

Pruning cane and bush berries. *Cane berries* all fall into two groups: those with rigid canes that grow upright, and those with trailing canes that tend to creep. Both types produce fruit on canes sprouted the previous year. Cut these canes to the ground as soon as you have harvested the crop. Leave about eight of the best new ones and cut the rest. Everbearing raspberries differ, in that a light crop forms at the tops of new canes in fall. Cut only the portion that fruits; the lower portion will bear the following year.

Rigid-caned berries include blackberry, blackcap raspberry, and purple raspberry. Cut old canes after harvest. Pinch young blackberry canes when they reach 36 inches. Pinch blackcaps and purple raspberries at 24 to 30 inches. Pinched canes will send out lateral growth. In winter cut blackberry laterals to 15 to 18 inches, and raspberries to 10 to 12 inches. Paint the bases white to distinguish them from summer growth. If you wish, tie the erect canes to a single wire stretched at 18 inches above ground.

Trailing raspberries. For single-crop berries, cut canes as soon as the harvest is over. Train new canes to a post, vertical wire, or horizontal supports. In summer, as new canes grow, gather them in bunches, tie them very loosely, and lay them along the ground until it's time for training. For everbearing raspberries, cut canes that fruit early in the season, and train young canes. These will fruit at the top in fall. Cut the fruiting portion after harvest, but leave the rest.

Trailing blackberries (dewberries) can be treated like raspberries. Another method is to stretch a wire 36 inches above the row of berry plants. After harvest remove old canes and cut off new ones at 48 inches. Canes that sprawl left are then pulled back to the right side of the wire. Canes that grow right are pulled to the left side. Tie if necessary. Extremely long laterals will grow outward, knitting together. Train them as needed along the wire.

Bush berries such as blueberries, currants, and gooseberries tend to bear very heavily if left completely unpruned. You can clean them up by removing the oldest shoots (3 and 4 years old) in winter, thinning out the worst tangles among the twigs, and cutting out dead wood. If berries are very small one year, thin the following winter. If they are large, skip the thinning.

Grape Spurs

Grape spurs do not form naturally like apple spurs. You create them by cutting back old canes each year to two buds. The resulting jagged small branch is called a spur. Not all grapes are pruned this way; some are cane-pruned.

Pruning grapes. Grapes all require heavy pruning to produce fruit, but different kinds need different pruning. Wine grapes and muscadines will usually need spur pruning, in which all side branches of a mature plant are cut to 2 buds in fall or winter. Two new shoots grow on the spur you leave and each produces a cluster or bunch of fruit.

Some grapes do not produce fruit on shoots that grow too near the main scaffold. 'Thompson Seedless' and many American grapes such as 'Concord' are among these. For these grapes you must cane-prune.

Instead of cutting to a short spur in winter, leave 2 whole canes from the previous growing season. When fruit forms from side growth along this cane, clip the cane off beyond the next set of leaves. You thereby encourage 2 new canes that will bear fruit the following year. Both spurs and canes grow from a permanent trunk, or trunk-plus-arms that you train on a trellis or arbor.

Third Dormant Season: Spur Pruning

Remove all shoots from the vertical trunk. Choose the strongest side shoots on horizontal branches and cut to two buds. Remove weak shoots at base, spacing two-budded spurs about 6 to 10 inches apart.

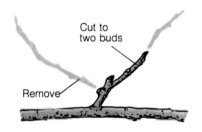

Cut to two buds

Remove

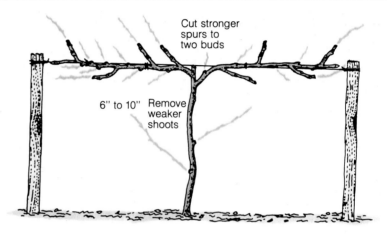

Cut stronger spurs to two buds

6" to 10" Remove weaker shoots

Annual pruning. Each dormant season after the third, each spur will have a pair of shoots that produced fruit during the summer. Cut the stronger to two buds. These buds will produce fruit-bearing shoots in summer. Remove weaker shoot. Repeat each year. Always keep trunk clear of growth.

Third Dormant Season: Cane Pruning

Remove shoots from trunk. Cut horizontal branches back so that two long shoots remain on each. On a two-wire trellis, you can leave up to eight shoots per vine. Tie the shoot farthest from the trunk to the trellis. Cut the other to two or three buds. The tied shoot will fruit the following summer. The clipped shoot will produce growth to replace it next winter, fruit the year after.

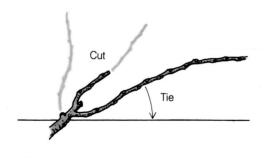

Cut

Tie

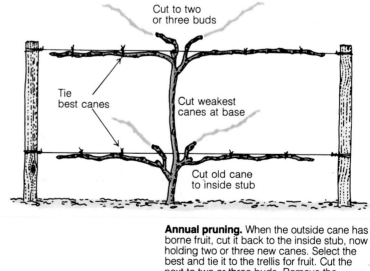

Cut to two or three buds

Tie best canes

Cut weakest canes at base

Cut old cane to inside stub

Annual pruning. When the outside cane has borne fruit, cut it back to the inside stub, now holding two or three new canes. Select the best and tie it to the trellis for fruit. Cut the next to two or three buds. Remove the weakest at the base. Repeat each year.

Pruning Spur and Cane Grapes for the First Three Seasons

When you plant. Plant a rooted cutting with two or three buds above the soil, then bury those in light mulch. Grapes root deep and need good soil.

First dormant season. Choose the best shoot and cut others to the base. Head remaining shoot to three or four strong buds.

Second dormant season. Cut away all side shoots, leaving only the trunk and two major branches. Tie these to the top of the arbor or trellis wire.

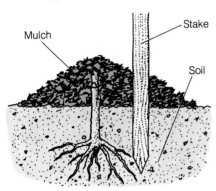

Mulch

Stake

Soil

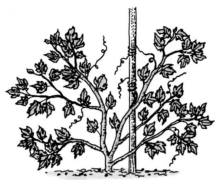

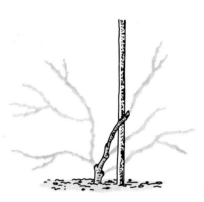

First growing season. Leave the plant alone. It will grow a number of shoots.

Second growing season. When new shoots reach about 12 inches long, select the most vigorous and pinch off others at the trunk. Tie the remaining shoot to a support (arbor post, trellis post). When the shoot reaches the branching point at the top of the arbor or trellis wire, pinch it to force branching. Let two strong branches grow, pinch any others at 8 to 10 inches long.

Third growing season. Let vine grow. Pinch tips of sprouts on trunk. After this, spur and cane pruning differ.

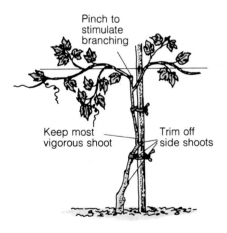

Pinch to stimulate branching

Keep most vigorous shoot

Trim off side shoots

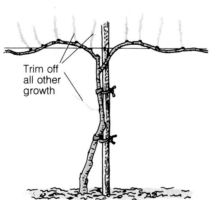

Trim off all other growth

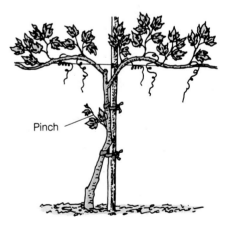

Pinch

The grape cultivar list in the "Encyclopedia of Fruits and Berries" (pages 126–132) indicates whether you should practice spur or cane pruning on a particular variety. In general, all muscadines need spur pruning. Americans of the 'Concord', or fox grape group need cane pruning. Wine grapes usually require spur pruning. For any grape not listed, check with your agricultural extension agent, or experiment by cane-pruning a portion of a mature vine, and spur-pruning another portion.

Additional special hints on pruning fruits and berries appear in the individual entries of the "Encyclopedia of Fruits and Berries."

Apples on M9 stock are trained at a 45-degree angle to induce early fruiting; the central leader operates like a lateral branch of a regular orchard tree. The number of fruiting spurs is increased by the bending and by summer and dormant pruning.

Espaliers take only a small area but provide a wealth of flowers and fruit.

Training

Fruit can be grown successfully as hedges, garden dividers, boundary plantings, and espaliers. This section details how you can use dwarf trees and training to confine fruit trees within tiny spaces.

Home gardeners are not the only ones concerned with limited-space planting. Commercial growers are experimenting with training methods that let them grow fruit in hedgerows and harvest their crops without having to haul ladders and climb 30 feet up a standard tree. The methods we outline here combine commercial experience with the classical training methods called *espalier* and *cordon* training.

Growing fruit in tight spaces is really no harder than maintaining a healthy rosebush, but keep the following points in mind: Be especially careful about planting and general maintenance. Prepare your soil well and, where drainage is a problem, use low raised beds. Feed and water on a regular schedule. Spray before damage occurs (some pests and diseases do their work before you can really see the results). Don't let new growth escape from you and spoil the pattern. Inspect your plants frequently.

In limited-space planting, training continues at all seasons throughout the life of the plant. Be ready to pinch or snip at any time. Major pruning is still a winter task, but in summer you must head, or cut away, wild growth and suckers, and you may need to loosen, renew, or add ties.

Be sure you understand the normal growth patterns of the plants you intend to train. For example, dwarf apples and pears grow slowly and bear fruit in the same places for years. Although fruiting spurs may need to be renewed over the years, the growth pattern means that you can confine these trees to very formal shapes and keep them that way. On the other hand, peaches and nectarines fruit on branches that grew the previous year. Old branches will not bear, so they should be cut away like berry canes and replaced with new growth from the base of the tree. This heavy pruning means that rigid training patterns are impossible. Peaches and nectarines can be fanned out over walls, or grown as hedges, but they cannot be held to strict geometric shapes.

In warm climates you may wish to try training a citrus. You can train them along wires for a fence, or espalier them on walls.

Grapes make good subjects for fences or walls, and a variety that requires a little more heat than your region normally offers may produce good fruit when grown on a south or west wall.

You can train cane berries flat against fences or walls, and treat them something like peaches, since you must replace all canes that have fruited with canes of the current season.

The poorest subjects for limited-space training are the quince and cherry. Quince fruits at the tips of new twigs, and cherry is normally too large to confine and will not fruit at all without a pollinator close by. Both of these plants can be trained, but your efforts would be better spent with something more rewarding.

Natural Training

Apples and pears. Both dwarf apples and pears grow and fruit well when trained as hedges against horizontal wires. Use wooden rails in very cold climates. Set posts about 8 feet apart. Stretch a bottom wire between them at 24 inches above ground. For very small trees, place the upper wire at 4 or 5 feet. For larger dwarfs, place a third wire at 6 or 7 feet.

Plant the young bareroot trees about 3 feet apart, beginning next to an end post. The last tree will go in about 2 to 3 feet short of the final post. If you buy unbranched trees, bend the trunk at a 45-degree angle and tie it to the wire. If there are any branches with wide crotches, cut them so only 2 leaf buds remain. Clip off those with narrow crotches at the trunk. Do not feed.

During the first season, train the trunk and any new branches at about 45 degrees, tying loosely where they touch the wires. Pinch off at the tip any branches that seem badly spaced, or that point at right angles to the fence—but wait until winter to do this.

The first winter, remove badly placed branches at the trunk. Remove the tips from well-placed branches, cutting to a healthy bud on the top of each branch. Feed lightly as growth begins.

The second summer continue training shoots at the ends of branches upward at 45 degrees. Cut side growth to 4 buds beginning in July. Feed lightly.

Each winter thereafter, remove tangled or damaged growth and cut remaining long shoots to 4 leaf buds. Feed as growth begins. Each summer, cut out suckers and excessively vigorous sprouts as they appear. Shorten new growth to four leaves from July on, and feed the trees in early August to encourage fruiting wood.

This training method allows side branches to grow outward, away from the fence. Your hedge will eventually become 3 to 4 feet wide. You can hold it at that width by pulling some of the outward growth back toward the fence with string, but check ties frequently or they will cut the branches. If parts of your hedge begin to escape and grow too far outward, trim them back to healthy side branches in May. To maintain the proper height of 5 to 8 feet, cut top growth back to a healthy side shoot near the top wire in May.

Training Apples and Pears

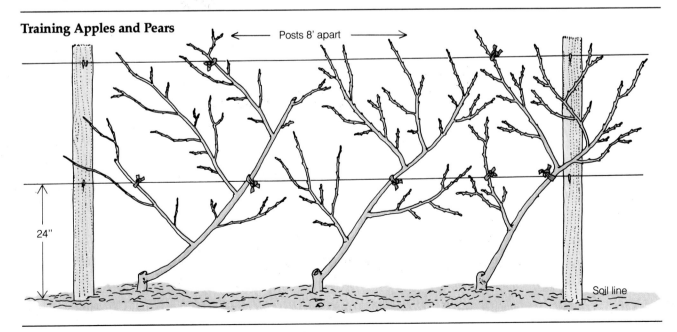

Training Peaches and Nectarines

Each year cut out branches that have born fruit, letting new branches replace them to bear next year's fruit.

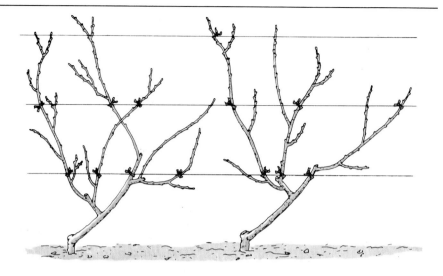

Peaches and nectarines. Since a peach hedge must have its fruiting wood renewed annually, you will need long replacement branches each year. For a hedge, plant as described under apples, using wires at 2, 4, and 6 feet. Cut the whips to about 24 inches long and shorten those side branches that point along the fence to two buds each. Cut off other branches at the trunk. Train all new growth at 45 degrees in both directions. Remove any suckers from below the bud union, cutting to the trunk.

The first winter, cut out about half the new growth at the base, choosing the weakest branches for removal. Cut off the tops of branches you retain, if they have grown beyond the hedge limits. Feed lightly as growth begins.

Fruit will form on the branches that grew the previous summer. The original trunk and the lowest branch will form an approximate V-shape at or below the lowest wire. During the second summer, choose the healthiest shoots from the lower portions of these main branches, and pinch back all other growth, especially growth above the second wire, after it produces six to eight leaves. The lower shoots will replace the entire upper structure and should be tied back loosely to the fence. Continue to remove suckers below the bud union, and feed lightly twice during early summer and midsummer.

When leaves drop in fall, cut out all branches that have fruited, and head back the V-shaped main structure to the middle wire. Paint all wounds with pruning compound and train the new growth to the fence. Feed as growth begins. During the summer, again encourage the lower shoots and pinch back the upper growth, feeding twice. Always be sure that new growth is above the bud union.

This training method will work well against a wall in cool regions where the wall will supply a little extra heat to ripen fruit. Form a wall-trained tree into a fan shape with the outer branches nearly horizontal, the central branches nearly vertical.

Apricots and plums. Use approximately the same technique described for peaches, but instead of replacing all growth each year, replace about a third and head back new growth on the remaining branches to four to six leaves during the summer.

Cane berries. Canes of the previous season can be trained to a fan or column shape against a wall or used as a fence on a two-wire trellis. (See cane berries under "Pruning," page 67.) New canes should be gathered into loosely tied bundles and placed lengthwise along the wall or fence until old canes fruit. After fruiting, cut out old canes and put the new ones in place. Where disease is a problem, as in many areas of the South, cut and destroy all canes

Cane Berries

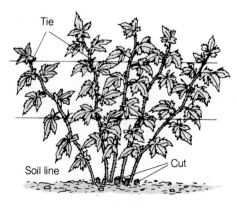

Tie

Soil line

Cut

immediately after fruiting and use late-summer growth for the following year's crop.

Grapes. With grape vines you have a choice of arbor training, cordon training, head training, or trellised canes. An arbor is an overhead frame on posts at least 8 to 10 feet on a side. Train a vine up each vertical post with two branches crossing the top horizontally. It may take more than two seasons to reach the top and begin training the horizontals.

Train each vine to either 2 or 4 cordons. For 4, allow 3 shoots to grow during the second growing season. Train 2 of the shoots horizontally, and tie the other vertically until it reaches the upper support, then pinch and select 2 horizontals.

A head-trained vine is freestanding but may not give much fruit. This method is attractive, and can be used for spur or cane grapes. Stake the young trunk and allow up to 4 shoots to grow, beginning about 24 or more inches above the ground. To spur prune, cut each shoot to 2 buds in winter each year. To cane prune, gather the fruiting canes upward and tie them together toward the tip. Let growth from renewal buds trail.

Trellised canes are grown on wire like a four-arm cordon, but the permanent wood is confined to short stubs near the trunk, and the fruiting canes are tied to the wire.

Formal Shapes

Only apples and pears can be trained in formal shapes, and pears may be a disappointment in regions where such diseases as fireblight are a problem. Some formal plants, with the training already started, are available from nurseries, and can be planted and maintained with no initial effort, but they are expensive.

The principle of formal training is simple: Encourage buds to grow at fixed places on a young tree, tie them in position as they lengthen, and then hold them in place by light pruning throughout the year.

A warning about any form of training: Ties must be checked frequently, since a tight tie will cut the branch and kill it. Don't tie branches directly to a support. Use a figure-8 tie: Tie a loose loop around the branch and then tie the loop securely to the support.

Espaliered trees may serve four purposes: they define property boundaries; they break up garden and lawn expanses; they esthetically enhance the landscape; and they provide a generous fruit harvest in limited space. These are dwarf 'Yellow Delicious' apples.

Encouraging bud growth. On any tree, the leaf buds farthest from the ground will grow best. On a horizontal branch, the buds on top will grow best, and those near the trunk will leaf out sooner than those near the tip. Note that branches grow most vigorously when vertical, and growth slows as a branch is bent toward horizontal. Cutting a branch forces bud growth below the cut. You can produce a similar effect by cutting a small notch in the bark just above a leaf bud. The bud below the notch will tend to sprout. You can weaken a bud by nicking bark just below it.

The three basic shapes that underlie all formal training are: *the straight vertical, the 45-degree angle,* and *the straight horizontal.* A single tree is trained in only one shape, but it can be repeated with several branches so that the tree has several vertical, angled, or horizontal members, as shown in the sketches below. A tree trained flat is called an *espalier.* Vertical training may be adapted to freestanding three-dimensional shapes.

Training vertical trees. A tree trained to a single stem without branches is called a *cordon.* Plant the young tree with the bud union about 2 inches above the soil surface. Cut side shoots to 2 buds. Train the tree against a wall, pillar, post, or wire trellis, but it must be on the south or west side.

Allow the tree to grow through the first summer with no further pruning. The first winter after planting, cut back the central leader by a third to a half, cutting the minimum amount if side growth is vigorous, more if it has grown weakly. More cutting will force more growth the following summer. New branches should be cut to 3 buds. New growth on older branches is cut to one bud.

The following summer, beginning in July, cut new branches to 3 buds, and new growth on previously trimmed branches to one bud. Do not cut the top vertical branch until it reaches the height you desire. An exception is if the tree fails to produce much side growth. Then cut new growth on the main stem by a quarter to a third in winter.

When the tree reaches the height you desire, clip the leader about 2 buds below that height in May. Thereafter, trim all new branches to 3 buds, and all new growth on old branches to 1 bud during the summer. In winter, trim any new branches you missed earlier. Feed and water carefully to prevent excessive growth.

Forming several vertical branches. To form a number of vertical branches on the same tree, you must encourage two or more buds on opposite sides of the trunk, then cut away the trunk above them. To be sure that the right buds grow, make use of bark notches.

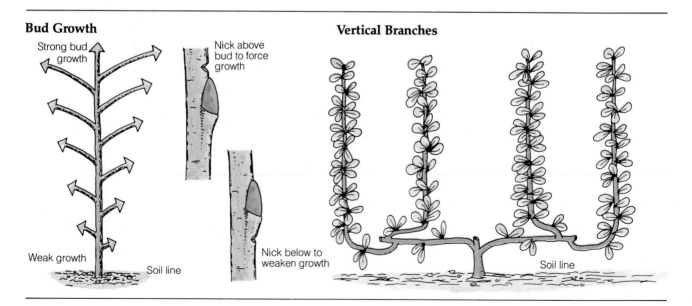

Bud Growth

Strong bud growth

Nick above bud to force growth

Weak growth

Soil line

Nick below to weaken growth

Vertical Branches

Soil line

Begin by finding two buds low on the trunk but above the bud union. They should be close together and pointing in opposite directions. Place a horizontal support (wire, wooden rail) an inch or two above the buds. If the support is fixed to a wall, the wall should face south or west.

Just above the lower bud, cut a small notch in the bark. Above the upper bud, nick the bark to the wood. Remove the next two buds entirely, then cut a deep nick in the bark just below the next higher bud. Snip off the trunk above this bud.

The effect will be as follows: The notch and nick above the lowest buds will force them into growth, because nutrients will stop at the cuts. The topmost bud will grow too, but weakly, because you have cut the bark below it. This last bud helps the tree to draw nutrients past the two buds you wish to keep.

In late summer, tie the new shoots from the lower buds to the horizontal support. If one is weaker, let it remain almost vertical. In winter, cut the trunk just above the pair of new branches. For a U-shaped tree, let the new branches grow vertically again after they form the bottom of the U. After the first season, treat them as you would a single vertical cordon. You can also train the new shoots at 45 degrees or horizontally. Pruning for these shapes is the same as for a vertical cordon.

To form a double U-shape, train the first two shoots into a broad U, becoming vertical when the branches are 2 feet apart. Let the verticals grow at least 2 feet up from the bottom support (they may require a second season). Repeat the notching and trimming as before on each vertical, training the buds into twin U's 1 foot across.

Espaliers. To form an espalier with a central trunk and a number of opposing branches, you will use a slightly different method. For the first pair of horizontal or angled branches, notch and nick two opposite buds below the encouragement, remove the next two, and cut off the trunk above the third. Continue for each pair of horizontals.

Three dimensions. For a three-dimensional shape the technique is the same, but you will encourage three or four closely spaced buds placed evenly around the trunk. Three buds will be divided again for six upright cordons; four buds will produce eight uprights. After shoot growth has begun, use a hoop or a square frame to train the horizontal portion of your tree. Use a hoop about 2 feet across for a simple vase shape. A pointed cone shape will require a hoop 3 feet across or, for eight verticals, a square frame 3 feet on a side.

Espaliers

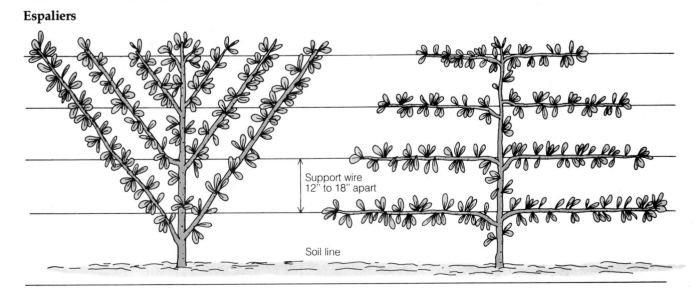

Support wire
12" to 18" apart

Soil line

Above: Espaliered trees alternate with fence posts to create a living fence.

Opposite: A small, well-pruned tree yields a full harvest.

Summer Pruning

Vigorous fruiting varieties will have to be controlled by frequent summer pruning. Summer pruning weakens a plant by removing leaves that manufacture nourishment, and within limited space, such pruning is the main means of confining trees. (Winter pruning has the opposite effect, causing a vigorous burst of spring growth.) Too much summer pruning, however, can damage a tree. How much pruning is necessary can best be learned from experience, but here are some guidelines.

In early summer, remove only excessively vigorous sprouts that threaten to take over the tree. These may suddenly shoot out much farther than any other growth. Cut them off at the base. Also remove any suckers from below the bud union, cutting to the base. Paint large wounds with pruning compound.

When the new growth matures and slows its pace, begin snipping it back. The season will vary—depending on weather, feeding, and watering—but by July you can begin with some branches, and finish up by early September. Cut off all but about four leaves of the current season's growth on each new branch. Then give your trees a last feeding of nitrogen to produce new fruiting wood. Don't thin out branches. You can do that during winter pruning if necessary.

If you find that one tree in a hedge or row regularly overgrows and escapes the pattern you have established, you would do well to remove this tree and plant a less vigorous one.

ENCYCLOPEDIA OF FRUITS AND BERRIES

This encyclopedia gives details of specific fruit types, growing seasons, and favored geographical locations.

The information in this encyclopedia is designed to help you choose the best possible fruits for your garden. Each entry contains notes on tree or plant size, planting, how the fruit grows, pruning and thinning, pollination, pests and diseases, and, where applicable, special tips on cultivation.

This is followed by cultivar lists that contain many of the best and most popular fruit varieties, selected to provide good choices in no matter what part of the country gardeners may live. Some cultivars are grouped by the time they are harvested relative to the growing season; for example, "Early," "Midseason," or "Late." Others are grouped by type of bearing, growth habit, or hardiness. You'll find information on where the cultivar originated (which may give you a valuable clue about how well it will do in your area), a description of the fruit and the plant, special growing requirements and other distinctive characteristics, and the best uses for the fruit once it's harvested. In addition, where possible we tell you in which section or sections of the country the cultivar performs best.

However, bear in mind that just because a fruit is recommended for one area does not necessarily mean that it can't do well in others. Climatic conditions vary so widely over the United States that any such recommendations must be general. Local geographical features and other factors that affect climate, as well as special treatment from the gardener (for example, providing sheltered areas or winter protection), can support plants that generally are not expected to do well in a given region. If you are attracted to a particular cultivar but are uncertain whether you can grow it in your garden, check with your local nursery staff, county extension agent, or gardening neighbors. Then, if you're still uncertain and can afford to take the chance, go ahead and plant it anyway. It can't hurt to try.

The numbers in parentheses following many cultivars correspond to our list of catalog sources on page 139 and 140. You can order the designated cultivars directly from many of these dealers. If the source is a wholesaler, you should order the varieties through your local nursery, who in turn should be able to get the plants you want from the wholesaler. After some numbers you'll see a capital "D" or "S." These mean that the dealer is offering dwarf or semidwarf plants.

FRUITS

Apples

For some people, the only apple is a polished red one. Others must have a red-and-yellow apple, or a golden one, or a tart green apple for pies. We've tried to allow for these preferences by presenting a broad selection of the most popular and most important apples for the home gardener. You'll find the popular cultivars such as 'Delicious', 'Jonathan', and 'McIntosh', and many of their sports. You'll also find the newest hybrids developed for special conditions and purposes.

Top: 'Johnee', a sport of the
'Jonathan' apple.
Right: 'Red Delicious' apple
Above: 'Golden Delicious' apple

There are well over a thousand apples available today. Many of these have been developed through the painstaking, time-consuming efforts of apple breeders. In breeding, each parent plant supplies half the heritage of the seedlings, but that half may contain a set of characteristics either partly or completely hidden in the parent. Seedlings are an uncertain entity, and breeders must grow them to fruiting size to see what characteristics they do have. This work takes time, and many seedlings prove to be inferior to their parent trees.

Sports, or mutations, may occur at any time, often without apparent reason: suddenly one branch of a tree is different. Occasionally the odd branch results from mechanical damage, such as pruning; sometimes experimenters purposely change genetic structure with chemicals or radiation. Most sports are worthless, but now and then one turns out to have characteristics that make it worth propagating to create a new strain.

One way to arrive at a general understanding of apple breeding is to look at those cultivars that serve as "heads of families." Three of these are 'Delicious', 'Jonathan', and 'McIntosh'.

'Delicious', which now is by far the most popular and economically important apple in America, first sprouted in an Iowa orchard in 1872. Its parentage is uncertain, but one parent may have been a nearby 'Yellow Bellflower' apple. That 'Delicious' exists at all today is almost a miracle. The owner, Jesse Hiatt, cut the seedling down twice; but it resprouted, and finally he let it grow. In about 1880 it bore fruit, which Hiatt thought was the best he'd ever tasted. The name 'Delicious' was given at a fruit show by C. M. Stark of Stark Nurseries. Stark didn't learn the name of the grower until 1894, but by then the apple had begun its rise to fame. 'Delicious' has produced a number of sports, including the redder-colored 'Richared', 'Royal Red', 'Hi Early', Chelan Red', and 'Red Queen'; and the spur-type 'Starkcrimson', 'Redspur', 'Wellspur', 'Hardispur', and 'Oregon Spur'. The original red sport was 'Starking'. 'Delicious' is also a parent of 'Melrose'.

The first seedling of 'Jonathan' sprouted in Kingston, New York, apparently from a fruit of an 'Esopus Spitzenburg'. A Judge Buel of Albany found the apple so good that he presented specimens to the Massachusetts Horticultural Society, naming it for the man who first showed it to him. 'Jonathan' was the primary variety before 'Delicious' took over.

Red sports of 'Jonathan' include 'Jon-A-Red' and 'Johnee'. Hybrid descendants include 'Jonagold', 'Jonamac', 'Idared', 'Melrose', 'Minjon', and 'Monroe'.

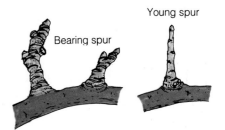

Young spur

Bearing spur

The 'McIntosh' apple came from the McIntosh Nursery in Ontario, Canada. John McIntosh discovered it about 1811, but did not propagate grafted stock until 1835, when the grafting technique was perfected. The variety became widely known in about 1900. Well-known descendants of 'McIntosh' include 'Summerred', 'Niagara', 'Early McIntosh', 'Puritan', 'Tydeman's Red', 'Jonamac', 'Macoun', 'Empire', 'Cortland', 'Spartan', and the spur variety, 'Macspur'.

Other apples with long lines of descendants include 'Rome', 'Golden Delicious', 'Northern Spy', and 'Winesap'.

The extensive work on dwarfing rootstocks for apples has produced plant sizes ranging from a 4-foot bush to a 30-foot spreading tree. There is even a true, or genetic, dwarf these days that stays small on any rootstock. (The subject is complex; you'll find a detailed discussion of comparative size on page 15.)

Dwarfing rootstocks make it easy for a gardener to control size even further by the special techniques outlined in this book. Apples can now grow in boxes, flat on a wall or trellis, as hedges, or in fanciful three-dimensional shapes.

Apples bear on long-lived spurs, so heavy pruning won't remove your crop. That means that any training method in these pages will suit any apple. See pages 70–75.

Apples are also among the easier fruit plants to graft, and a beginner can feel like an expert when he succeeds in producing a multiple-variety tree on the first try.

The sketch will show you how an apple spur looks and bears. The fruit forms at the tip of last year's spur growth, and the spur itself then grows a bit more, off to the side of the fruit. Each spur bears for 10 years or more, so don't tear it off when you pick. For comparison, the straight spur at the right has not yet borne fruit.

You will hear about spur varieties. These are sports of standard cultivars. They grow more slowly than regular plants, and their spurs are packed closer together on the branch. This less vigorous growth means that they are a kind of genetic dwarf, but they are still good-size trees unless grafted to dwarfing roots. Spur cultivars are difficult to train formally. If you buy spur varieties on dwarfing roots, use an informal training method that doesn't call for any particular form.

Pruning methods depend on how you grow the tree. For special training, turn to page 70. For general pruning of the larger dwarfed trees or standard trees, see the section on pruning beginning on page 56.

Thinning is crucial with many apple cultivars. If left alone, they overset, and the heavy crop can snap branches. Even more important, many apple cultivars tend to bear every other year. If you leave too much fruit you tend to encourage alternate bearing, and the year following a good crop you may find that your tree bears only a handful of apples.

There are many thinning methods, but the most direct is to wait for the natural drop of young fruit in June, then thin the remaining fruit so there is one every 6 inches along the branches. Each spur may have a cluster of fruit. A single fruit is less likely to become diseased, so leave only the largest fruit on each spur. Thin carefully, or you will damage the spurs.

Apples are only partially self-fertile, but many cultivars set a good crop without a pollinator. Any two kinds that bloom together offer cross-pollination (with the exceptions listed below). If you plant only a very early and a very late variety, they will not cross-pollinate.

Throughout the seasons, this espaliered 'Gravenstein' apple needs care. Top, left to right: The tree breaks into bud and then into full bloom. As the buds break (center), spray to lessen susceptibility to scale and scab.

Bottom: Spray for codling moth after the petals have fallen (left). Thin the fruit when it is thumbnail size to one per spur (center) to ensure a well-formed harvest.

A few apples are completely self-sterile. The following will not set a crop at all if you plant them together with no other source of pollen: 'Gravenstein', 'Stayman' (and 'Stayman' sports such as 'Blaxstayman' and 'Staymared'), and 'Winesap'.

All apples need some cool winter weather, but as there is great range in this requirement, choices are available for any climate except subtropical and low desert regions.

Apples are subject to attack by many organisms, but the gardener will have most trouble with codling moth and other fruit-spoiling pests, and then with the usual aphids, mites, and scale. See pages 49–55 for further details. A regular spray schedule is best. A fungicide will control diseases such as mildew and scab where they are a problem.

Early season cultivars. 'Early McIntosh'. Origin: New York. A 'McIntosh' cross with 'Yellow Transparent', the fruit has a good red skin and is excellent eaten fresh, in sauce, and in pies. However, the tree is difficult for the average grower to thin and prune. (24DS, 26, 34DS, 44DS)

'Gravenstein'. The fruit is large but not uniform, with skin that's red against light green. The greenish yellow flesh is moderately fine-textured, crisp, firm, and juicy. The tree is strong, very vigorous, upright, and spreading. Excellent for eating fresh, in sauce, and in pies. Widely available.

'Lodi'. Origin: New York. The fruit is up to 3 inches in diameter, with light green skin, sometimes with a slight orange blush. The flesh is nearly white with a greenish tinge, fine-grained, tender, and juicy, but sour. The eating quality is only fair, but 'Lodi' is excellent in sauce and pies. The tree tends to overset fruit and must be thinned early. Widely available.

'Yellow Transparent'. Introduced from Russia almost 100 years ago, this apple is still valued by a loyal following as an early green cooking apple. It is medium size with greenish yellow skin. The texture is fine-grained, crisp, and juicy. It bruises readily and soon becomes overmature. It is good fresh and excellent for sauce and pies. Widely available.

Early to midseason cultivars. 'Jonagold'. Origin: New York. A cross of 'Jonathan' and 'Golden Delicious', this is a beautiful large apple with a lively yellow-green ground color and bright red blushes. Cream-colored flesh is crisp and juicy, with good flavor. It is good for cooking and among the very best for fresh eating. Stores well. The trees are vigorous and sturdy, with wide-angled branches. (26S, 27, 31D, 44DS)

'Jonamac'. This 'McIntosh'-type dessert apple is of very good eating quality, milder in flavor than the 'McIntosh'. (27, 44DS)

'Jonathan'. Origin: New York. The standard 'Jonathan' is one of the top cultivars grown in commercial orchards in the Central States. The fruit is medium-size and uniform; the skin is washed red and pale yellow; and the flesh is firm, crisp, and juicy. Rich flavor makes it a good choice for snacks, salads, and all culinary uses. Trees bear heavily. Widely available.

'Paulared'. Origin: Michigan. This apple rates high on several counts. It is attractive in color—a solid red blush with a bright yellow ground color. The flesh is white to cream and nonbrowning. Excellent, slightly tart flavor makes it good for eating fresh and in sauce and pies. Although it colors early, for quality apples it should not be picked until nearly mature. Fruit holds well on the tree and is harvested in two pickings; it has a long storage life. The tree is everything an attractive tree should be—strong, upright, with good branch structure. (21DS, 41DS)

'Tydeman's Red'. Origin: England. A 'McIntosh' type, similar in shape and ripening four weeks earlier, this apple is almost entirely red from a very early stage. Fruits should all be picked within a few days for optimum quality and flavor, and because they drop quickly at maturity. They are good eating quality and keep much longer than most early varieties. Early ripening, when few other varieties are being harvested, is a virtue. One drawback is growth habit—the branches are undesirably long and lanky, and need to be controlled by pruning. For best results, grow on dwarf or semidwarf rootstocks. Widely available.

Midseason cultivars. 'Empire'. Origin: New York. This cross between 'McIntosh' and 'Delicious' has medium, uniform fruit with dark red, striped skin and whitish cream flesh that is firm, medium-textured, crisp, and very juicy. Eating quality is excellent. A major fault is that it develops full color long before maturity, tempting the grower to harvest too early. Trees are moderately vigorous and of upright-spreading form. (1S, 2S, 26S, 27, 31D, 41DS, 44DS)

'Macoun'. Origin: New York. This cultivar received a new burst of interest in the early 1970s because of its excellent quality when eaten fresh. A cross of 'McIntosh' and 'Jersey Black', it resembles 'McIntosh' but is smaller. Skin is very dark red in color; flesh is white, richly flavored, aromatic, and of high quality as a dessert fruit. The tree grows upright with long, lanky branches. Thinning aids in attaining good fruit size. Widely available.

'Wealthy'. This hardy old-timer is good for eating and cooking. A long bloom period makes it a good pollinator for most other midseason cultivars. Fruit is medium to large, uniform, and rough. Flesh is white stained with pink, and fine-textured, firm, tender, tart, and juicy. It is good fresh and for pies, baking, and stewing, and excellent for sauce. Widely available.

Midseason to late cultivars. 'Cortland'. Origin: New York. According to many apple growers, this is excellent—even better than 'McIntosh'—as a dual-purpose apple, for eating and cooking. The tree bears heavy crops of large red-striped fruit with white flesh which, when exposed to air, is slow to turn brown, making it especially suited for use in salads. The

'Jonagold' apple, a cross between 'Jonathon' and 'Golden Delicious'.

'Jonamac' apple

'Tydeman's Red' apple

'Cortland' apple

'Cortland' apple

'Red Delicious' apple

'Golden Delicious' apple

tree is strong and very vigorous, with a spreading, drooping growth habit. Widely available.

'Delicious'. The most important apple grown in the United States, the fruit is medium in size, long and tapering in shape. The skin is striped-to-solid red with slightly yellow flesh that is firm, juicy, sweet, and aromatic. Hand thinning is usually necessary to produce apples of good size and dessert quality. Widely available.

'Idared'. A cross of 'Jonathan' and 'Wagener', this hybrid has an attractive, nearly solid red skin with a smooth finish. Of large, uniform size, it has white, firm, smooth-textured flesh that is excellent for eating fresh and for cooking. It has a long storage life. The tree is strong, vigorous, upright, and very productive. Widely available.

'McIntosh'. If you write down the attributes of a great apple—medium to large fruits, white flesh, sweet, tender, juicy; very good eaten fresh, in sauce, in pies, or as a cider variety—you would have the 'McIntosh'. The skin is yellow with a bright red blush. The tree is strong and very vigorous. Widely available.

'Newtown Pippin'. This is a midseason-bordering-on-late cultivar. The fruit is medium in size with greenish yellow skin and crisp, firm flesh. It is good for eating fresh, and excellent for sauce and pies. The tree is strong and vigorous. Widely available.

'Rhode Island Greening'. Still rated at or near the top as a cooking or processing cultivar after more than 200 years, this apple is light green to yellow, firm-fleshed, crisp, and juicy. It is a top quality choice for sauces and baking. The tree generally produces good crops but is a poor pollinator. It bears in alternate years. (22, 24DS, 26S, 27, 31DS, 41DS)

Late cultivars. 'Golden Delicious'. For a great eating and cooking apple, 'Golden Delicious' ranks as high as any. The fruit is medium to large and uniform in size. The skin is greenish yellow with a bright pink blush. The flesh is firm, crisp, juicy, and sweet—excellent fresh and in desserts and salads, and very good for sauce. The tree is medium in height, moderately vigorous, upright, and round, with wide-angled crotches. It bears very young and bears annually if thinned. Widely available.

'Granny Smith'. This apple is imported from Australia and New Zealand for sale here. The fruit is medium to large. The flesh resembles 'Golden Delicious', a bright glossy green, but is more tart in flavor. It is very good eaten fresh, in desserts, salads, sauce, and pies. The tree is strong, vigorous, upright, and spreading. Widely available.

'Mutsu'. Origin: Japan. A cross of 'Golden Delicious' and the Japanese 'Indo', this relative newcomer has gained the approval of both growers and consumers. Large, oblong, greenish fruits develop some yellow color when mature. The flesh is coarse-textured, firm, and crisp. The flavor is excellent (more tart than 'Golden Delicious') when eaten fresh, and it is rated high for sauce, pies, and as a baked apple. Unlike 'Golden Delicious' it does not shrivel in storage. The tree is very vigorous and spreading. Widely available.

'Northern Spy'. Trees of this cultivar are very slow to come into bearing; sometimes 14 years elapse before they produce their first bushel. The fruit is large, with yellow and red stripes, and the flesh is yellowish, firm, and crisp. The quality is excellent fresh and for pies. The fruit bruises easily, but has a long storage life. Trees are vigorous and bear in alternate years. Widely available.

'Red Delicious'. This is the number-one supermarket apple. There is no question about its dessert and fresh-eating quality. The fruit is medium to large in size, with skin color striped to full red. The flesh is moderately firm in texture and very sweet and juicy. Your best choices are the red sports such as 'Wellspur', or 'Royal Red'. The tree tends to produce full crops every other year unless properly thinned for annual bearing. Widely available.

'Rome Beauty'. Origin: Ohio. This cultivar and its sports are known as the world's best baking apples. Many red sports (such as 'Red Rome') are available with a beautiful, solid, medium-dark-red color. The fruit is large and round, and flesh is medium in texture, firm, and crisp. The tree is moderately vigorous, comes into production at an early age, and is a heavy producer. The fruit has a long storage life. Widely available.

'Spartan'. Origin: British Columbia. This is a cross between 'McIntosh' and 'Newton'. The fruit is medium in size, uniform, and symmetrical in shape, with a solid dark red skin. Flesh is light yellow, firm, tender, crisp, and juicy. It is strictly a dessert variety. The tree is strong, moderately vigorous, and well shaped. It must be thinned to assure good size and annual bearing. Widely available.

'Stayman'. Origin: Kansas. This variety is a very late ripener. Where it can be grown, it is good for cooking or eating fresh. The fruit is juicy with a moderately tart, rich, winelike flavor. The skin is bright red and the flesh is fine in texture, firm, and crisp. Skin cracking is one drawback. The tree is medium-size and moderately vigorous. Widely available.

Extra hardy cultivars. In cold-winter areas where some of the favorite apples are subject to winter damage, three hardy cultivars developed by the University of Minnesota stand out.

'Honeygold'. Origin: Minnesota. This apple boasts a 'Golden Delicious' flavor. The fruit is medium to large with golden to yellow-green skin and yellow flesh that is crisp, smooth, tender, and juicy. It is good for eating fresh and in sauce and pies. The tree has a moderately vigorous growth habit. (11)

'Red Baron'. Origin: Minnesota. This cross of 'Golden Delicious' and 'Red Duchess' has round, medium-size fruit with cherry red skin. The flesh is crisp and juicy with a pleasantly tart flavor. It is good eaten out-of-hand, or in sauce and pies. (11)

'Regent'. Origin: Minnesota. This cultivar is recommended for a long-keeping, red winter apple. The fruit is medium in size, with bright red skin

Top: 'Rome Beauty' apple
Above: 'Mutsu' apple

Top: An apricot tree, if well cared for, may bear fruit for 15 to 20 years.

Above: Harvest apricots when the fruit is firm and ripe.

and creamy white, juicy flesh of crisp texture. Rated excellent for cooking or eating fresh, it retains its fine dessert quality late into winter. The tree has a vigorous growth habit. (11D, 41DS)

Cultivars for Southern California. 'Beverly Hills'. Early. This is a small- to medium-size apple, striped or splashed with red over a pale yellow skin. The flesh is tender, juicy, and tart. Overall, the apple resembles 'McIntosh'. Use it fresh or cook it in sauce or in pies. The tree is suited mainly to cooler coastal areas. Heat spoils the fruit. Locally available.

'Winter Banana'. Midseason. The large fruit is strikingly beautiful. The skin color is pale and waxy with a spreading pink blush on the sunny side. The flesh is tender with a fine, special aroma and tangy flavor. 'Winter Banana' requires a pollinator such as 'Red Astrachan' in order to set a good crop. Locally available.

For other varieties that can be grown in your area, consult your local nursery or agricultural extension agent.

Apricots

In the colder regions of the country, the selection of apricot cultivars is limited, since they bloom early and may suffer frost damage. In recent years, however, a number of hybrids with hardy Manchurian apricots have been produced to fill the gap, and now varieties, such as 'Moongold' and 'Sungold', will fruit fairly regularly even in the northern plains. The choice of varieties widens in milder regions, and more tender varieties, such as 'Moorpark', will bear in the eastern states.

Even the dwarfed apricots on special rootstocks produce fair-size trees, and a full-size tree will fill a 25-foot-square site; but you can train the tree to branch high and use it in the landscape as a shade tree.

Apricots, like plums, bear on spurs that produce for 2 to 4 years and then need to be pruned out and replaced with younger wood. See the sketch on this page. Fruit may form in the second year, but don't expect a heavy crop until the third or fourth year. Trees are fairly long-lived and may last from 15 to 30 years, depending on location and care.

Many apricots are self-fertile but in colder regions it is usually best to plant a second variety for pollination to encourage the heaviest fruit set possible. Frost damage may remove many of the young fruits.

In pruning apricots, you need to head back long new whips by half and remove the oldest fruiting wood. Generally, thinning is natural, either from frost or from natural drop in early summer. If your tree sets very heavily, you will get larger apricots by thinning to 2 inches between each fruit. For pruning details, see page 64.

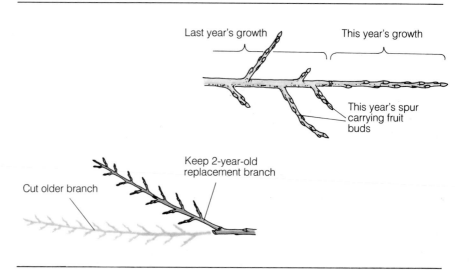

Last year's growth

This year's growth

This year's spur carrying fruit buds

Keep 2-year-old replacement branch

Cut older branch

Apricots can flourish in landscape settings but require deep watering to soak the roots thoroughly.

Apricots can also be used as stock plants for grafts. Plums do well on apricot stock, and peaches may take, although the union is weak. Your apricot tree can bear several different fruits over a long season when you mix grafts.

Brown rot and bacterial gumming are serious pests.

Cultivars. Check for climate adaptability and pollinating requirements, and be sure to buy hardy trees in the colder regions.

'Earligold'. Origin: California. This is a medium-size fruit with rich golden skin and juicy flesh. The tree is a heavy producer and requires little winter chill. Begins ripening in mid-May. Good for Southern California. Locally available.

'Early Golden'. This medium to large, pale yellow fruit is blushed red, with smooth skin and fine flavor. It ripens in mid-August in New York. Good for the North and South. (2D, 4D, 8, 12, 16D, 22D, 26)

'Hardy Iowa'. Origin: Iowa. This variety is a hardy chance seedling sold by the propagator. The fruit is pale yellow and rather small, with thin skin and very sweet flesh. Good for fresh fruit, or pie and preserves. The tree is a prolific bearer and flowers late, escaping frost. Good for the North. (12)

'Moongold'. Origin: Minnesota. A hybrid with 'Manchu' as one parent. The same cross also produced 'Sungold', and the two must be planted together for pollination. The fruit is orange with tough skin. The flesh is orange-yellow and of very good quality. The tree is a spreading, medium-size plant. Fruit ripens in Minnesota in late July before 'Sungold'. Good for all zones. (11, 13D, 16, 19, 25, 32, 34)

'Moorpark'. Origin: England. This cultivar, dating from 1760, is considered by many to be the standard of excellence among apricots. The large fruit is orange with a deep blush, sometimes overlaid with dots of brown and red. The flesh is orange, of excellent flavor, and has a pronounced and agreeable perfume. Ripening is uneven, with half the fruit still green when the first half is already ripe. This is an advantage in the home garden, since the gardener does not have to use the fruit all at once. The tree does well in all but the most extreme climates. Widely available.

'Newcastle'. This apricot is for areas with mild winters. The fruit resembles 'Earligold' and is medium in size. The tree requires little chilling and bears in June. Good for the South. Locally available.

'Perfection' ('Goldbeck'). Origin: Washington State. The fruit is very

Below: 'Moongold' apricot
Bottom: 'Moorpark' apricot

'Sungold' apricot

large, oval and blocky, and light orange-yellow without a blush. The flesh is bright orange and of fair quality. The tree is vigorous and hardy, but blooms early and so is uncertain in late-frost areas. Since it requires little winter chill it will grow in mild-winter areas. It needs a separate pollinator. In the Southwest use another early variety. Good for the South and West. (2, 4, 18D, 19, 32D, 34D, 41)

'Riland'. Origin: Washington State. The fruit is large and rather flat. The light yellow skin is covered over half the fruit by a deep blush. The flavor is rich and plumlike, but the texture is somewhat coarse. The tree is vigorous and upright and requires a pollinator. Good for the West. (7, 34)

'Scout'. Origin: Manitoba. This cultivar originally came from a Manchurian fruit experiment station. The flat, bronzy fruit is medium to large with deep yellow flesh. It is good fresh and can be canned or used in jams. The tree is tall and upright, vigorous, and hardy. Fruit ripens from late July. Good for the West. (16)

'Sungold'. Origin: Minnesota. A selection from the same cross as 'Moongold', this apricot must be planted with 'Moongold' for pollination. The fruit is rounded and of medium size, with a tender, golden skin blushed orange. The flavor is mild and sweet, and the fruit is good fresh or preserved. The tree is upright, vigorous, and of medium size. The fruit ripens somewhat later than 'Moongold'. Good for all zones. (11, 13, 16, 19, 25, 26D, 30)

'Wenatchee'. The fruit is large and has a flattened oval shape with orange-yellow skin and flesh. The tree does well in the Pacific Northwest. Good for the West. (7, 18, 34D, 40)

Cherries

Cherries come in four distinct forms, with many cultivars in each. The *sweet cherry* sold in markets is planted commercially in the coastal valleys of California and widely in the Northwest, especially Oregon. There are also extensive commercial plantings near the Great Lakes. All cherries require some winter chilling, which rules out planting in the mildest coastal and Gulf climates; but they are also damaged by early intense cold in fall, and where rainfall is heavy during ripening. Sweet cherries are especially tricky for the home gardener, but try them wherever summer heat and winter cold are not too intense. *Sour cherries*, or *pie cherries*, are more widely adapted and are good in cooking and canning. These are the most reliable for home gardeners, and there are many cultivars developed for special conditions. The dwarf 'Meteor' and 'Northstar' pie cherries were developed for Minnesota winters. These, 'Early Richmond', and 'Montmorency' all can withstand both cold and poor spring weather better than sweet cherries. *Duke cherries* (hybrids) share sweet and sour characteristics. In areas with extremely cold winters, try the Hansen bush cherry, a group of selections from the *Nanking cherry*.

Cherries come in many sizes. Bush varieties reach 6 to 8 feet tall and spread about as wide. The dwarf sour cherries grow to about 8 feet, but have a single trunk. Standard-size sour cherries and sweet cherries on dwarfing roots both reach 15 to 20 feet. A standard sweet cherry is the largest and can equal a small oak in size, if the climate permits. Such cherries can serve as major shade trees.

All cherries bear on long-lived spurs. Those on tree cherries can produce for 10 years and more, and begin to bear along 2-year-old branches. Count on the first crops in the third or fourth year after planting. Bush cherries may bear sooner.

Sweet cherries need a pollinator, with the exception of 'Stella'. 'Windsor' is a good pollinator and bears well, but always plant at least two cultivars, or use a graft on a single tree. Sour cherries are self-fertile, as are the bush cherries.

Cherries need no thinning, and little pruning after the first two seasons of growth. See page 62 for methods of developing wide crotches, and apply them to young sour cherries. Sweet cherries may need heading back in the first years of growth to encourage branching (see page 64).

The bush cherries and dwarf pie cherries make fine hedges and screens, with lovely bloom and a good crop. Larger cherries can be grafted for a choice of fruit and good pollination.

Birds are the major pests, but cherries also need protection from fruit flies, pear slugs (actually an insect larva), and bacterial gumming. See pages 49–55.

Check pollination requirements carefully if you plant a sweet cherry. For any cherry, check the recommended climate area. If you try a cherry outside its zone, offer as much protection as possible in fall and winter.

Early cultivars. 'Black Tartarian'. This medium-size black cherry is fairly firm when picked, but softens quickly. It is widely planted because it is one of the earliest cherries, and an excellent pollinator. Trees are erect and vigorous. Use any sweet cherry as a pollinator for many others. Good for all zones. Widely available.

'Sam'. Origin: British Columbia. This medium-to-large, black-fruited cherry is firm, juicy, and of good quality. The fruit resists cracking and the tree is very vigorous, bearing heavy crops. Use 'Bing', 'Lambert', or 'Van' as a pollinator. Good for the North and West. Widely available.

Midseason cultivars. 'Bing'. This variety is the standard for black sweet cherries. The fruit is deep mahogany-red, firm, fleshy, and very juicy. It is subject to cracking and doubling. The tree is spreading and produces heavy crops, but suffers from bacterial attack in humid climates. It is not easy to grow, but is popular. Use 'Black Republican', 'Sam', 'Van', or 'Black Tartarian' (*not* 'Napoleon' or 'Lambert') as a pollinator. Good for all zones. Widely available.

'Chinook'. Origin: Washington State. This is a 'Bing'-type fruit, large and heart-shaped, with mahogany skin and deep red flesh. The tree is spreading, vigorous, and a good producer. It is slightly more hardy than 'Bing'. Use 'Bing', 'Sam', or 'Van' as a pollinator. Good for the West. (7, 40)

'Corom'. Origin: Oregon. This cultivar is the recommended pollinator for 'Royal Ann' in the Pacific Northwest. It is a yellow cherry with a blush, and thick, sweet, quite firm flesh. It is moderately resistant to cracking and is a good canning cherry. The tree is fairly vigorous. Use 'Royal Ann', 'Sam', or 'Van' as a pollinator. Good for the West. Locally available in the Pacific Northwest.

'Emperor Francis'. This large, yellow, blushed cherry resembles 'Napoleon', but is redder and more resistant to cracking. The flesh is very firm. The tree is very productive and hardier than 'Napoleon'. Use 'Rainier', 'Hedelfingen', or 'Gold' (*not* 'Windsor' or 'Napoleon') as a pollinator. Good for the North. (1, 2, 4, 8, 22, 26, 27, 33, 41DS)

'Garden Bing'. This genetic dwarf plant remains only a few feet high in a container, but grows to perhaps 8 feet in the ground. It is self-pollinating and bears 'Bing'-like dark red fruit. Good for the West. (37)

'Gold'. Origin: Nebraska. This is a yellow cherry that is highly resistant to cracking. Tree and blossoms are especially hardy and very productive. The tree withstands −30°F. Fruit of the original strain is small, but some strains are larger. Use any sweet cherry as a pollinator. Good for the North. (33, 41DS)

'Governor Wood'. Light yellow with a red check, this cherry is large and rounded with tender, fine-textured flesh. Use 'Black Tartarian', or a pie cherry as a pollinator. Good for the South. Locally available.

'Kansas Sweet' ('Hansen Sweet'). Origin: Kansas. This is not really a sweet cherry, but a fairly sweet form of the pie cherry group. The fruit is red, with a firm flesh that is good fresh as well as in pie. The tree and blossoms are hardy in Kansas. It is self-fertile. Good for the North. (6, 12, 19D)

'Black Tartarian' black cherry

French 'Royal Ann' (also called 'Napoleon') yellow cherry

'Stella' black sweet cherry

'Lambert' black cherry

'Rainier'. Origin: Washington. In shape, this cherry resembles 'Bing', but is a very attractive blushed yellow, with firm, juicy flesh. The tree is vigorous, productive, and spreading to upright-spreading. It is particularly hardy. Use 'Bing', 'Sam', or 'Van' as a pollinator. Good for the South and West. (9DS, 18, 27, 34)

'Royal Ann' ('Napoleon'). This very old French variety is the standard for yellow, blushed cherries. It is the major cherry appearing in commerce as candy and maraschino cherries. The firm, juicy fruit is excellent fresh and good for canning. The tree is very large, extremely productive, and upright, spreading widely with age. The tree is relatively tender, although the buds tolerate some cold. Use 'Corom', 'Windsor', or 'Hedelfingen' as a pollinator (*not* 'Bing' or 'Lambert'). Good for all zones. Widely available.

'Schmidt'. Origin: Germany. 'Schmidt' replaces 'Bing' as a major commercial black cherry in the East. The fruit is large and mahogany-colored, with thick skin. The wine-red flesh is sweet but somewhat astringent. The large, vigorous tree is upright and spreading. It is hardy, but the fruit buds are fairly tender. Use 'Bing', 'Lambert', or 'Napoleon' as a pollinator. Good for the North and South. Widely available.

'Stella'. Origin: British Columbia. This is the first true sweet-cherry that is self-fertile (requiring no pollinator). The fruit is large, dark in color, and moderately firm. The tree is vigorous, fairly hardy, and bears early. It can be used as a pollinator for any other sweet cherry. Good for the South and West. (7, 9DS, 16, 32D)

'Van'. Origin: British Columbia. This large, dark fruit has some resistance to cracking. The tree is very hardy and especially good in borderline areas, since it has a strong tendency to overset, and therefore may produce a crop when other cherries fail. It bears from 1 to 3 years earlier than 'Bing'. Use 'Bing', 'Lambert', or 'Napoleon' as a pollinator. Good for all zones. Widely available.

'Yellow Glass'. This is an especially hardy variety with clear yellow fruit the size of a pie cherry, but sweet. Use 'Black Tartarian' as a pollinator. Good for the North. (6, 16, 19, 25)

Late cultivars. 'Black Republican' ('Black Oregon'). This cherry is firm and very dark with some astringency. The tree is quite hardy, but tends to overbear heavily, producing small fruit. In borderline areas it may produce where others fail. Use any sweet cherry as a pollinator. (7S, 9S, 34)

'Hedelfingen'. Origin: Germany. The variety bears dark, medium-size fruit with meaty, firm flesh. Resists cracking, but some trees sold under this name are not crack-resistant. The tree is only moderately hardy, has a spreading and drooping form, and bears heavily. As a pollinator, use any sweet cherry listed here. Good for the North and South. (1, 2, 22, 27, 33, 41DS)

'Lambert'. This large, dark cherry ripens later than 'Bing' but is similar. The tree is more widely adapted than 'Bing', but bears erratically in many eastern areas and is more difficult to train and prune. The strongly upright growth produces weak crotches if left untrained. Use 'Van' or 'Rainier' as a pollinator (*not* 'Bing', 'Napoleon', or 'Emperor Francis'). Good for all zones. Widely available.

'Windsor'. This is the standard late, dark commercial cherry in the East. The fruit is fairly small and not as firm as 'Bing' or 'Lambert'. It is, however, very bud-hardy and can be counted on to bear a heavy crop. A fine choice for difficult borderline areas where others may fail, the tree is medium-size and vigorous with a good spread. For a pollinator, use any sweet cherry except 'Van' and 'Emperor Francis'. Good for the North and South. Widely available.

Bush cherry cultivars. Bush cherries are attractive, many-stemmed shrubs derived from two separate sources: the Nanking cherry, an Asian species; and the native Western sand cherry. They are ornamental as well as fruit-

producing, but require long periods of cold weather. The fruit, borne in heavy crops, is somewhat plumlike.

Left: 'Montmorency' sour cherry
Above: 'Bing' black sweet cherry

Hansen bush cherry. Origin: South Dakota. The fruit is dark to red, depending on the selection, and the plant begins bearing in the first year after planting. The shrub is an excellent ornamental, with heavy bloom, and reaches 4 to 5 feet tall with an even broader spread. Use the fruit fresh, in cooking, or in preserves. Good for the North. (2, 8, 12, 13, 16, 22, 26, 28)

Western sand cherry. Many improved cultivars are sold, with fruit ranging from black to red to yellow. All bear heavily and are attractive in flower: 'Black Beauty'. Black fruit. (12, 16); 'Brooks'. Maroon fruit. (12, 16); 'Golden Boy'. Yellow fruit. (12); 'South Dakota'. Deep red fruit. (12)

Duke cherries. The Dukes are hybrids between sweet and pie cherries. They have tart, acid fruit like pie cherries, but are large, fairly upright trees like sweet cherries.

'Late Duke'. This large, light red cherry ripens in late July. Use it for cooking or preserves. In cold climates it requires a sour cherry pollinator. In mild climates it is self-fertile. Good for the West. (34)

'May Duke'. A medium-size, dark red fruit of excellent flavor for cooking or preserves. In cold climates, use an early sweet cherry for pollination. In mild climates it is self-fertile. Good for the West. (34)

Sour (pie) cherry cultivars. The following varieties are all self-fertile. They will pollinate sweet cherries in mild-climate areas. There are two types: the amarelle, with clear juice and yellow flesh; and the morello, with red juice and flesh. In the coldest northern climates, the amarelle is the commercial cherry.

'Early Richmond'. An amarelle, the fruit is small, round, red, and excellent for pie, jam, and preserves. It is astringent when eaten fresh. The tree reaches 15 to 20 feet tall. Good for all zones. Widely available.

'English Morello'. This late-ripening morello cherry is medium-size, dark red, and crack-resistant. The tart, firm flesh is good for cooking and canning. The tree has drooping branches and is small and hardy, with only moderate vigor and productivity. Good for the North. (27)

Below: 'Barbara Ann' crab apple
Bottom: 'Siberian Crab' crab apple

'Meteor'. Origin: Minnesota. This amarelle is a genetic dwarf that reaches only about 10 feet tall. The fruit is bright red and large for a pie cherry, with clear yellow flesh. The tree is especially hardy, but does well in milder climates too, and is an ideal home garden tree for all cherry climates. Good for all zones. Widely available.

'Montmorency'. This amarelle is the standard sour cherry for commercial and home planting. The large, brilliant red fruit has firm yellow flesh and is strongly crack-resistant. The tree is medium to large, vigorous, and spreading. Various strains have slightly different ripening times and fruit characteristics. Good for all zones. Widely available.

'Northstar'. Origin: Minnesota. This is a genetic dwarf morello, excellent for the home garden. It has red fruit, red flesh, and resists cracking. The tree is small, attractive, vigorous, and hardy, and resists brown rot. Fruit ripens early but will hang on the tree for up to 2 weeks. Good for all zones. Widely available.

Crab Apples

Fine for jellies or pickled whole fruit, crab apples are also the most decorative of fruit trees. Flowers range from red to pink-and-white. Leaf color may be red, bronze, variegated red-green, or green. Fruits are of many sizes, from tiny cherrylike crabs to large, yellow, pink-cheeked kinds. The cultivars sold for flowers have edible fruit, but large-fruited kinds are better if your aim is to grow the fruit for jelly.

Crab apples range from small, 10-foot trees to spreading trees 25 feet tall. The large-fruited kinds are larger trees.

Crab apples fruit on long-lived spurs, generally producing clusters of several fruits on each. Since crops are heavy, you can cut back new wood without losing anything.

Crab apples are self-fertile, but you can graft several kinds that bloom at different times to extend the flowering season.

Train the young trees to a vase shape with three or four scaffolds. After the second year you can leave them alone or cut them back to maintain size. No thinning of the crop is necessary.

Use small varieties if you're crowded. If you have no space but want a light crop for jelly, graft a branch to an existing apple tree.

Crab apples are subject to the same diseases as apples, and scab is a major problem for some cultivars. Choose resistant kinds.

Cultivars. We include both large-fruiting kinds and those that are mainly ornamental, but also offer a good crop of smaller fruit. Use red or pink fruits if you want pink jelly.

'Barbara Ann'. This ornamental offers dark reddish purple, ½-inch fruit with reddish pulp. The tree produces a profusion of 2-inch purple-pink, full double flowers. It grows to about 25 feet tall and is reasonably disease-resistant.

'Chestnut'. This very large, bronzy-red crab apple is big enough to make a good dessert or lunch-box fruit, and can also be used to make a deep pink jelly. Its flavor is especially pleasing. The tree is very hardy, medium-size, and reasonably disease-resistant. (11, 16)

'Dolgo'. The smallish, oblong red fruit is juicy, and if picked before fully ripening, it jells easily, making a ruby-red jelly. The tree is hardy, vigorous, and productive. Fruit ripens in September. Widely available.

'Florence'. The large yellow fruit has an attractive red blush. Use it for pale pink jelly or for whole-fruit pickling. The tree is medium-large and somewhat tender, so it is best planted in warmer regions. It ranges from fairly to very productive. Widely available.

'Hyslop'. This fair-size fruit is yellow blushed with red. Use it for whole relishes, or for pale pink jelly. The tree is fairly hardy and quite ornamental, with single pink bloom. (6, 13, 33, 41)

'Katherine'. The tiny fruits of this cultivar are yellow with a heavy red blush, and are very attractive on the tree. They can be made into a pink jelly. The tree is small, slow-growing, and fairly hardy, but it flowers and fruits every other year. It reaches about 15 feet tall and is reasonably disease-resistant. The 2-inch flowers are fully double, opening pink, then fading to white.

'Montreal Beauty'. This medium-size green crab apple with red striping will serve for jelly or as a base for mint or rose geranium jellies. The tree is medium to large, hardy, and fairly disease-resistant. Locally available.

'Profusion'. These tiny scarlet fruits are good in jellies. The tree spreads only slightly, is small (to about 15 feet), and produces small single flowers that are deep red in bud, and then open to purplish red to blue-pink. It is moderately susceptible to mildew.

'Siberian Crab'. This cultivar bears an abundance of clear scarlet, medium-size fruit that can be jellied or pickled whole. The tree is vase-shaped and reaches 15 to 30 feet tall, depending on climate and soil. The inch-wide white flowers are fragrant. There are disease-resistant forms of this tree and those which are subject to infection.

'Transcendent'. These large yellow crab apples are blushed with pink on one side. Use them for clear jellies, or eat them fresh if you like the wild, astringent flavor. The tree is medium to large and somewhat disease-resistant, but not very hardy, so plant in warm areas. (7, 18, 34)

'Whitney'. An old favorite, this cultivar has very large fruit, good for fresh eating, jelly, preserves, or apple butter. The color is yellow with red stripes. The tree is hardy, medium to large, and reasonably disease-resistant. Widely available.

'Young America'. A fairly new cultivar, this large and abundant red fruit makes a clear red jelly with a splendid flavor. The tree is especially vigorous and hardy, and ripens fruit about mid-September. (27)

Top left and right: 'Dolgo' crab apple produces abundant large flowers.
Above left: 'Katherine' crab apple
Above right: 'Profusion' crab apple

A fig tree adds its elegant form to a landscape.

'Brown Turkey' fig

Figs

Although the fig is generally thought of as a subtropical fruit suited mainly to the mild winters and heat of the Gulf coast regions, California, and the southwestern desert areas, there are some varieties that will bear even in the milder climates of the Northwest and the Northeast. If a freeze knocks the plant down, it sprouts again quickly.

Figs are good fruit for gardeners who don't want to fuss with spraying and pruning, but like to see a big crop on their tree. In warm regions the fig bears big, juicy fruit in early summer, then sets a heavier crop of small fruit, perfect for drying, in fall. It lives for many years, loves clay soil if drainage is good, and needs next to no attention. You have a choice of red-fleshed, dark fruit or bright pink-fleshed, greenish yellow fruit.

In cold-winter regions, fig shrubs reach 10 feet tall and spread that much or more. In warm regions, trees grow to 15 to 30 feet and spread wide and low. You can easily cut them back or confine them.

Figs are not really fruits in the botanical sense. They are a collection of inside-out flowers with all the important parts accessible to the outside world only through a hole at the base. The first crop "blooms" on new wood of the previous season, and the second crop appears on new wood of the current season. When a tree is cut back to confine it, you usually lose most of the first crop. You also lose it in cold regions where winter does your pruning.

Most home-garden cultivars need no pollination. The California commercial fig, 'Calimyrna', does need pollinating and should not be planted in the South.

No fruit thinning is necessary. Prune the young tree to an open shape in the first two years, then remove any suckers at the base when you think about it. Pull—don't cut—them. Shrub forms need no attention except for removing dead wood.

You can prune a fig to a 5-foot spreading shrub if you like, or flatten it on a south wall. They can also be grown as a container plant for use on a patio or to allow them to be protected by moving them to a garage or storage area.

Figs need no attention to pests or disease.

Cultivars. Favorites are 'Mission' and 'Brown Turkey', but you may want a cultivar that appears less frequently in the market.

'Adriatic'. The fruit is green-skinned with a strawberry-colored pulp. In hot areas, the second crop has a paler pulp, and in cool-summer areas the fruit of both crops is larger. This is principally a drying fig. The tree is vigorous and large. 'Adriatic' is recommended for California. It is locally available.

'Brown Turkey' ('Turkey', 'Southeastern Brown Turkey', 'San Piero', 'Black Spanish'). A large-fruited cultivar for fresh use. The first crop is large and dark brown; the second crop is smaller. The pulp is light strawberry. The tree is small and can be pruned heavily to cut the crop. One of the hardiest cultivars, it is worth trying in the Northeast and Northwest. Recommended for Southeast and Southwest. (2, 14, 18, 35, 38, 42)

'Celeste' ('Blue Celeste', 'Celestial', 'Sugar', 'Malta'). Bronzy fruit with a violet tinge. The pulp is amber with rose tones. 'Celeste' is the most widely recommended fig in the Southeast, but is also grown in the West. An especially hardy plant. (2, 35, 38)

'Conadria'. Origin: California. One parent is 'Adriatic'. The fruit is thin-skinned and white with a violet blush, with white to red flesh that resists spoilage. The tree is vigorous and precocious, producing two crops. Recommended for the hot valleys of California. Locally available.

'Kadota' ('Florentine'). Fruit is tough-skinned and greenish-yellow, and the first crop has a richer flavor. This is principally a canning and drying cultivar. The tree is strong-growing. Recommended for hot California valleys. (37, 42)

'King' ('Desert King'). The fruit is green with flecks of white; the pulp violet-pink. The tree comes back from the roots after a freeze and bears in fall. Recommended for Oregon fig climates. Locally available.

The first crop of a 'Mission' fig ripens as the second crop appears.

'Latterula'. This large greenish yellow fig with honey-colored pulp also called the white Italian honey fig, grows on a very hardy tree that bears two crops. Recommended for Oregon fig climates. Locally available.

'Magnolia' ('Brunswick', 'Madonna'). This is a large straw-colored fig on a fairly hardy tree. Recommended for the Southeast. (2)

'Mission' ('Black Mission'). This cultivar bears two heavy crops of black fruit with deep red pulp. The first crop has larger fruit; the second crop can be dried. The tree is large and vigorous. Recommended for California and desert regions, but also grown in warmer Southeastern zones. (37, 42)

'Texas Everbearing' ('Dwarf Everbearing'). The fruit and tree resemble 'Brown Turkey'. This cultivar will re-sprout and bear after a freeze kills back the top. Recommended for Southeast and South Central. (2, 5, 6, 12, 13, 35, 38)

Also check the local availability of 'Granata', 'Negronne', and 'Neveralla' in Oregon, and 'Genoa' ('White Genoa') on the California coast.

In the Southeast, also check for the local availability of 'Green Ischia' and 'Hunt'.

A low-chill peach cultivar will produce fruit in climates warmer than the prime peach-growing areas.

Peaches and Nectarines

Peaches. The peach is rightly one of the most popular of homegrown fruits. Both peaches and nectarines are at their best when tree-ripened, so a home gardener's time and effort are rewarded by a product that money can't buy.

Peaches cannot tolerate extreme winter cold or late frost, so in the northern plains states and northern New England, peaches are purely experimental. The hardiest, such as 'Reliance', may survive and bear in a protected spot, but you can't be sure. In more temperate climates near the Great Lakes, peaches do well; but choose the warmest site available for planting. A protected sunny spot where cold air can't collect and sit is the right place for your tree.

Some of the greatest peach-growing country in the world is in the West: California alone produces 50 percent of the commercial peaches in the United States. The San Joaquin Valley in California and areas of eastern Washington have the climate to produce great peaches: 200 to 1,000 hours of cold winter weather (around 45 degrees or below in December and January), warm and dry spring weather, and hot summers. Gardeners outside this prime area can grow satisfactory fruit by selecting the right cultivars for their own gardens. For warmer climates, selected low-chill cultivars can fruit well everywhere but in southern Florida.

The standard tree on a peach rootstock grows to about 18 feet tall and 15 feet wide and then stays there because it is best pruned heavily each year to maintain that size and to encourage lots of new growth along the branches. A semidwarf tree on Nanking cherry or St. Julien plum rootstock stays at 7 to 9 feet tall, and also needs the proper maintenance pruning to maintain size while encouraging new growth. The true, or genetic, dwarf peaches grow only about 4 to 6 feet tall and require no pruning to maintain size or force growth. At most, you will clip out tangles and remove broken twigs, and they are a good choice for patio container plantings.

Last year's growth now bearing fruit · This year's growth now forming next year's buds

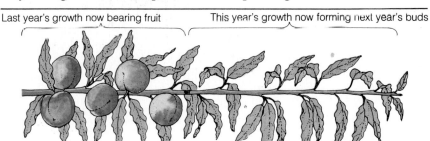

You won't have any trouble fitting a peach to whatever space is available to you. Among commercial growers of standard trees, the trend these days is toward the hedgerow, a narrow wall of trees formed by training the young trees to a V-shaped scaffold, then pruning to hold all growth within the hedge shape. This means trimming a bit in summer as well as pruning in winter, but it's not difficult. Just clip any runaways that shoot beyond the general hedge outline to about 8 to 10 leaves long. See page 71 for a trellis version of the same V-shape.

Semidwarf peaches are ideal for hedgerows and trellises and lend themselves well to another simple technique that is the home gardener's specialty. Dig an extra-big planting hole and set two to four varieties together, with their roots almost touching. You'll get the effect of a single small tree with several kinds of fruit. Of course, you can practice multiple planting with standards, too.

Fruit growth. The sketch above shows you the most important thing about a peach tree: It illustrates where on the branch you'll find flowers and fruit. Notice that fruit is formed only on branch segments that grew the previous summer. New wood grows on beyond the fruit and will produce next year's crop. Once fruit is harvested, the section of branch on which it grew will never fruit again. That's why you need to encourage new growth for replacement branches.

How do you encourage new growth on your standard or semidwarf trees? By pruning. As you prune you thin, head back, and remove weak branches. The tree responds with lush growth. See page 65 for details and a sketch of cuts to make.

Once a crop sets on a peach tree, you may not even see the branches through the fruit. And for three reasons, you can't leave it all: It will be too small; it slows branch growth; and it may snap branches. Thin it out when it reaches thumbnail size. For an early peach, leave 6 to 8 inches of space between each fruit; for a late peach, thin after the June fruit fall, and leave 4 to 5 inches between each fruit. If a frost knocked off much of your crop, leave all the rest, even if they're clustered. What is important is the ratio of leaf surface to number of peaches, so a sparse crop will do equally well in singles or bunches.

Peaches are twiggy trees, but the greatest number of flower buds form on sturdy new branches that made more than 10 inches of growth the previous summer. Keep these and thin the more anemic twigs. You can head the strong ones back by a third to a half if you want to keep the tree small. They'll bloom on the remaining half.

Only a few peach varieties need a pollinator. ('J. H. Hale' is one of the best known self-sterile cultivars.) Normally the trees are self-fertile, although bees are a big help in pollen transfer.

All peaches need winter rest. Without it, they bloom late, open their leaves erratically, and finally die. Check the chart for cultivars that suit your climate. Southern California peaches are listed as such. Some peaches have been bred for short, mild winters and may bloom too early or freeze in the North. Be sure to buy hardy, high-chill cultivars for the North. Chill is an important factor in the South as well. A high-chill peach will leaf out and flower erratically in southern Mississippi, while a low-chill peach may try to bloom before the last frost in Tennessee.

The universal peach ailment is leaf curl, but you can control it easily with a copper spray. See page 53 for control methods. You will also probably encounter the peach tree borer, gnawing the trunk at ground level. Brown rot attacks fruit but is controllable. For bacterial spot on leaves, check the list for resistant cultivars. Brown rot and plum curculio are the chief problems in the North.

Very early cultivars. 'Desert Gold'. Origin: California. This medium-size, round fruit has yellow skin with a red blush. The flesh is yellow, firm, and semi-freestone. The tree is fairly vigorous and productive. Good for the West, and particularly Southern California. (33D, 37D, 42)

'Springtime'. Origin: California. The small- to medium-size fruit has yellow skin with a high blush and abundant short fuzz. The flesh is white and semi-freestone. Good for the West, particularly Southern California. (42)

'Tejon'. Origin: California. The medium-size fruit is yellow with a red blush over half its surface; light fuzz. The yellow flesh is semi-freestone. The tree bears very well. Good for the West, particularly Southern California. Locally available.

Early cultivars. 'Blazing Gold'. Origin: California. The skin is blushed, and the yellow freestone flesh has reddish streaks near the pit. Flavor is slightly acid. The vigorous and productive tree has somewhat showy flowers and bears regularly. Good for the West. (37)

'Candor'. Origin: North Carolina. An outstanding cultivar for its season, this is a medium-size semi-freestone. The skin is bright red over a yellow ground. The flesh is yellow, fine-textured, and nonbrowning. It is productive and good for canning. The foliage has moderate resistance to bacterial spot. Good for the South. (2, 10, 17, 27D, 33, 41DS)

'Dixiered'. Origin: Georgia. This medium-size cling peach usually es-

Brown rot is one of the chief peach pests in northern regions. Spray as the fruit ripens.

For mild climates choose an early white peach.

capes spring frost damage. The skin is bright red, and the flesh is yellow, flecked with red; firm, fine-textured, and nonbrowning. The tree is vigorous and consistently productive. Good for the South. (2, 10D, 17, 18D, 34, 37, 38)

'Earlired'. Origin: Maryland. This is a medium-size cling peach. The skin is blushed red over yellow, and the flesh is yellow, firm, and medium-textured. Thin early and heavily. It is moderately susceptible to bacterial spot. Good for the South and West (very early in the West). (1, 2, 7, 17, 34)

'Erly-Red-Fre'. Origin: Virginia. This large, semi-freestone, red peach has white flesh. The tree is vigorous, hardy, and gives average production. It is resistant to bacterial spot. Good for the South. (1, 2D, 35)

'Fairhaven'. Origin: Michigan. For western Washington, this large peach is bright yellow with an attractive red cheek and light fuzz. The freestone flesh is yellow with red at the pit, and firm. It is a good freezer. The tree has showy flowers. Good for the West. (7, 34)

'Garnet Beauty'. Origin: Ontario, Canada. This variety is an early sport of 'Redhaven'. Medium-large, semi-freestone fruit hangs on the tree until overripe. Flesh is yellow streaked with red, firm, and slightly fibrous in texture. The tree is very vigorous and hardy and produces heavy crops that achieve good size and color even inside the tree. It is susceptible to bacterial spot. Good for the North. Widely available.

'Golden Jubilee'. Origin: New Jersey. An old standby, this medium-large freestone has skin mottled bright red. The flesh is yellow, firm, and coarse in texture. The tree is very hardy and sets heavy crops, but is self-thinning. Good for all zones. Widely available.

'Redhaven'. Origin: Michigan. One of the finest early peaches, this medium-size freestone is widely recommended. The skin is deep red over a yellow ground. The flesh is yellow, firm, melting, and nonbrowning. Fruit sets heavily and is good for freezing. The tree is spreading, vigorous, and highly productive. It resists bacteriosis. Good for all zones. Widely available. *Note:* 'Early Redhaven' is nearly identical, but two weeks earlier. (7, 10, 34)

'Redtop'. Origin: California. This peach will grow in Southern California. The large fruit is nearly covered with an attractive blush and light fuzz. The yellow freestone flesh is unusually firm and good canned or frozen. The tree is moderately vigorous and somewhat susceptible to bacterial spot. Flowers are showy. Good for the West. (7, 37)

'Reliance'. Origin: New Hampshire. A promising home-garden cultivar, this tree is very winter hardy: It will withstand −20 to −25°F. in January and February and still produce a crop that same year. The large freestone fruit has dark red skin over a yellow ground. The flesh is bright yellow, medium firm, and slightly stringy. Flowers are showy. Good for the North and West. Widely available.

'Sunhaven'. Origin: Michigan. Medium-large freestone. The skin is bright red over golden ground. Short, soft fuzz. The flesh is yellow flecked with red, firm, fine textured, nonbrowning. The tree is vigorous, consistently productive. Recommended for all zones. Widely available.

'Veteran'. Origin: Ontario, Canada. A favorite in western Washington and Oregon, the medium-to-large fruit is yellow splashed with red and has medium fuzz. The nearly freestone flesh is yellow and soft. The tree is vigorous and highly productive—one of the very best in cool Pacific climates. Good for the West. (7, 27, 34)

Midseason cultivars. 'Babcock'. Origin: California. The name 'Babcock' is often applied to a range of early white peaches, especially in the market. The small-to-medium fruit is light pink, blushed red with little fuzz. The skin peels easily. The nearly pure white flesh is red near the pit, tender, juicy, and of mild flavor. The medium-to-large tree is spreading and vigorous. Good for the West, particularly Southern California. (37D, 42D)

'Veteran' peach

'Early Elberta' (Gleason strain). Origin: Utah. This large freestone matures 3 to 10 days before 'Elberta'. The flesh is yellow and is considered of better flavor than 'Elberta'. It is good for canning and freezing. The tree is hardy and gives consistent production. Good for the South and West. Widely available.

'Glohaven'. Origin: Michigan. This large freestone peach has skin that is red over deep yellow. The flesh is yellow, firm, and nonbrowning. It cans and freezes well. Flowers are medium size and deep pink. The tree is vigorous and hardy. The fruit remains on the tree when mature. Good for the North. Widely available.

'J. H. Hale'. The skin of this extra-large freestone is deep crimson over a yellow ground, and nearly fuzzless. The flesh is golden yellow and firm. This cultivar needs cross-pollination for best production. Good for all zones. Widely available.

'Halehaven'. Origin: Michigan. The skin of this medium-large freestone is dark red over a yellow ground. The flesh is yellow, firm, and melting. The tree is vigorous and productive. It is susceptible to brown rot. Good for all zones. Widely available.

'July Elberta' ('Kim Elberta'). Origin: California. This cultivar is best suited for the Willamette Valley. The medium-size fruit is greenish yellow blushed and streaked with dull red, and very fuzzy. The yellow flesh is of high quality. The tree is vigorous and bears heavily but is susceptible to bacteriosis. Good for the West. (33, 37)

'Loring'. Origin: Missouri. This medium-size freestone has skin with slight fuzz and is blushed red over a yellow ground. The flesh is yellow, firm, medium in texture, and melting. It is a dependable cropper, setting fruit under adverse weather conditions, and resists bacteriosis. Good for the North and South. Widely available.

'Redglobe'. Origin: Maryland. Very adaptable to many peach-producing areas, this variety is above average quality for canning and freezing. A

Left: Many fruiting peaches have large, showy flowers.
Above: 'Early Elberta' peach

medium-large freestone, its skin is bright red over yellow ground, and the flesh is yellow, firm, fine in texture, and melting. It is a dependable producer. Showy flowers are deep pink. It is susceptible to bacterial spot. Good for the South and West. Widely available.

Late cultivars. 'Blake'. Origin: New Jersey. This large freestone has red, slightly fuzzy skin. The flesh is yellow, firm, and melting. The fruit hangs well on the tree, which is vigorous and productive, but sometimes erratic. 'Blake' is good for freezing, excellent for canning. It is susceptible to bacteriosis. Good for the North and South. (1, 2, 10, 17, 35, 41DS)

'Cresthaven'. Origin: Michigan. The skin of this medium-large freestone is bright red over a gold ground and almost fuzzless. The flesh is yellow and nonbrowning. The tree is hardy, and fruit stays on when mature. It is good for canning and freezing. Good for the North and South. Widely available.

'Elberta'. This large freestone is the old standard bearer for a midseason crop. The skin is red blushed over a deep golden yellow ground. The fruit tends to drop at maturity. The slight bitterness around the pit is preferred by many. It is resistant to brown rot. Good for all zones. Widely available.

'Georgia Belle'. Origin: Georgia. This is an outstanding white peach. The skin is red blushed over creamy white. The flesh is white and firm. The tree is vigorous, hardy, and productive, but very susceptible to brown rot. This peach has excellent flavor and is fair for freezing, but poor for canning. Good for the North and South. Widely available.

'Jefferson'. Origin: Virginia. Especially suited to localities where late spring frosts are a problem, this peach is noted for its fine texture and flavor. The skin is bright red over a bright orange ground. The flesh is yellow and firm. It is a reliable producer that cans and freezes well. It has some tolerance to brown rot. Good for the North and South. (1, 2, 10, 17, 27D, 35)

'Jerseyqueen'. Origin: New Jersey. This large freestone peach is bright red over a yellow ground. The flesh is yellow and firm. Flowers are showy, and the tree is productive. Good for the North and South. Widely available.

'Madison'. Origin: Virginia. Adapted to mountain areas of Virginia, this cultivar has exceptional tolerance to frosts during the blossoming season, setting crops where others fail. The skin of this medium-size freestone fruit is bright red over a bright orange-yellow ground. The flesh is orange-yellow, very firm, and fine in texture. The growth of the tree is average to vigorous. Good for the North and South. Widely available.

'Rio Oso Gem'. Origin: California. The skin of this large freestone is red over a yellow ground; the flesh is yellow, firm, fine in texture, and nonbrowning. Blossoms are light pink, very large, and showy. The tree is productive. Good for the South and West. Widely available.

'Sunhigh'. Origin: New Jersey. This medium-large freestone is very good in its season. The skin is bright red over a yellow ground. The flesh is yellow and firm. The tree is vigorous and spreading. It is very susceptible to bacteriosis and requires thorough summer spraying. Good for the North and South. Widely available.

Nectarines. The nectarine is simply a fuzzless peach. Peach trees sometimes produce nectarines as sports, and nectarine trees will produce fuzzy peach sports. Therefore the two plants are nearly identical, but nectarines are generally more susceptible to brown rot. In the South, gardeners may have trouble with the disease wherever hot, humid weather encourages it. You will have to spray regularly to control it. In climates where spring and summer are warm and moist, both blossoms and fruit must be sprayed to control brown rot. Otherwise, nectarines require the same care as peaches.

Early cultivars. 'Independence'. Origin: California. This medium-size oval fruit has brilliant cherry-red skin. The freestone flesh is yellow and firm. The tree is productive and moderately vigorous, with showy flowers. It will take warm winters. Good for the South and West. (2, 17, 37, 41DS)

'Pocahontas'. Origin: Virginia. The medium-to-large, oval fruit is a highly colored red. The semi-freestone flesh is yellow, slightly stringy, and of good quality. This cultivar resists brown rot and frost during the blossoming season, which makes it a good choice in northern areas. Good for the North and South. (2, 8, 10, 13, 17, 35)

'Silver Lode'. Origin: California. The skin of this fruit is red. The freestone flesh is white and sweet, and of good texture. The tree requires little chilling. Good for the South and West. (42)

Midseason cultivars. 'Fantasia'. Origin: California. This fairly large fruit has bright yellow skin covered up to two-thirds with a red blush. The freestone flesh is yellow, firm, and smooth. The tree is vigorous and productive, with showy flowers. It requires little winter cold. Good for the South and West. (2, 7, 14, 37, 41DS)

'Flavortop'. Origin: California. The large oval fruit is mostly red, with firm, smooth, freestone, yellow flesh. The tree is vigorous and productive, with showy flowers, and needs moderate winter cold. Good for the South and West. (2, 7, 41DS)

'Garden State'. Origin: New Jersey. The large fruit has a rounded oval shape. The skin is greenish yellow, almost completely covered with red. The yellow freestone flesh is firm and juicy. The tree is vigorous and spreading, with large showy flowers. Good for all zones. (2D, 7D, 8, 22, 34D)

'Gold Mine'. An old cultivar. The large white fruit is blushed red. The juicy white freestone flesh has an excellent flavor. It requires little winter chill, and ripens late in July or early in August. Good for the West. (37)

'Le Grand'. Origin: California. The large fruit has yellow skin with a light red blush. The flesh is firm and yellow. The large, spreading tree is productive, with large, showy flowers. Good for the West. (34, 37D, 42)

'Nectared 4'. Origin: New Jersey. The fairly large fruit is yellow with a red blush over much of the surface. The semi-freestone flesh is yellow. The tree is productive, with showy flowers. Good for the North and South. (13, 17, 27, 41DS)

'Nectared 5'. Origin: New Jersey. The large fruit is smooth, with a blush covering most of the skin. The undercolor is yellow. The flesh is semi-freestone until fully ripe, then freestone. The color is yellow and the tree is productive. Good for the South. (8, 13D, 17)

'Panamint'. Origin: California. The fruit has a red skin, and the freestone flesh is yellow. The tree is vigorous and productive and needs little winter chilling. Good for the South and West. (37, 42)

'Pioneer'. Origin: California. The fruit has a thin red skin. The freestone yellow flesh is of a rich and distinctive flavor, with red near the pit. The tree requires little chill and has large, showy bloom. Good for the West. Locally available.

'Sunglo'. Origin: California. One of the highest quality nectarines, this heavy-bearing variety requires heavy thinning and extra nitrogen for best performance. The fruit is medium-size freestone, with skin that's bright red over golden orange. The flesh is firm and melting. Good for the North. (33D)

Late cultivars. 'Cavalier'. Origin: Virginia. The medium fruit is orange-yellow with splashes and mottles of red. The yellow freestone flesh is firm, aromatic, and slightly bitter. The vigorous and productive tree has showy flowers and is highly resistant to brown rot. Good for the North. (2, 17, 35)

'Freedom'. Origin: California. This very large fruit has a highly blushed skin. The golden yellow freestone flesh is firm, juicy, and good for canning or dessert. The tree is medium-size, spreading, and productive, and the flowers are large and pink. Good for the West. Locally available.

'Redchief'. Origin: Virginia. This medium fruit is bright red and attractive. The flesh is freestone, white, and fairly firm. The tree is vigorous and productive, with showy flowers, and is very resistant to brown rot. Good for the South. (2D, 17, 18D, 34D, 35)

Nectarines are smooth-skinned sports of regular peaches.

Above: Genetic dwarf nectarines add beauty to a garden. They have heavy spring blossoms and beautiful winter silhouettes.

Top right: 'Bonanza' dwarf peach

'Stanwick'. An old cultivar, the large pale green fruit has red cheeks and white, juicy, freestone flesh of fine flavor. Use it for drying, canning, or freezing. The fruit tends to drop before fully ripe. The tree has large flowers. Good for the West. (37)

Genetic dwarf peaches and nectarines. The genetic dwarf peaches and nectarines form dense small trees, with long leaves trailing in tiers from the branches. In spring the branches are entirely hidden in flowers that are usually semidouble and always very showy. In winter the bare plants are also visually interesting. The fruit of all these plants is of normal size, sometimes large.

In containers, the plants can be kept to about 3 feet tall, but in the ground they will eventually reach 6 to 8 feet and spread widely. They can be used as ornamentals and require little care beyond spraying for the usual maladies of peaches.

Most require little winter chilling for good bloom, and none are blossom-hardy in really cold places, but they can be grown in containers and protected until the warm season. If you try this method in the coldest northern regions, you may have to pollinate the flowers yourself with an eraser, touching it first to pollen, then to the stigma of a flower.

These dwarf plants were created by breeding numerous cultivars together, but they all probably share the common heritage of the Swatox peach or the Flory peach, naturally dwarf Chinese cultivars.

Only the hardiest can go in the ground. Use them in containers.

Genetic dwarf peach cultivars. 'Bonanza'. Origin: California. This is one of the oldest and best known dwarfs. The medium-size fruit has a moderately red skin. The freestone flesh is yellow and ripens early. The tree needs moderate winter chill. The showy flowers are pink and semidouble. Good for all zones. (12, 32, 42)

'Compact Redhaven'. Origin: Washington. Unlike other dwarfs, this peach is a chance sport resembling 'Redhaven' in everything but size. It grows with leaf nodes close together and reaches about 10 feet tall. It will take more cold than other dwarfs and grows where 'Redhaven' grows. Good for all zones. (2, 12, 21, 33)

Genetic dwarf nectarine cultivars. 'Golden Prolific'. Origin: California. The large fruit has yellow skin, mottled orange. The freestone yellow flesh is red near the pit, soft, and of fair to good quality. The tree needs considerable winter chill. Very showy flowers. Good for the South and West. (6)

'Nectarina'. Origin: California. The medium-size fruit is yellow, blushed red. The yellow freestone flesh is red at the pit and of good quality. The tree needs little chilling, and the fruit ripens in mid- to late July. Good for the South and West. (42)

Pears

Pears, and especially dwarf pears, are a fine choice for the home gardener. The trees are attractive even in winter, they require little pruning after they begin to bear, and the fruit stores fairly well without any special requirements. The plants take well to formal or informal training, so space is no problem.

The one real drawback with pears is fireblight, but a home gardener can work around it by choosing cultivars wisely, or by replacing plants if that becomes necessary. Dwarf pears come into bearing fairly quickly. Fireblight is at its worst in spring when insects carry it from tree to tree. Resistant plants are the best answer. Cut off any infected tissue well below the infection and burn it. Other pests are codling moth and pear slug. See page 49–55.

Standard pears will spread 25 feet across and grow as tall or taller. A dwarf in natural shape needs a space about 15 feet square, but with the training methods listed in this book you can grow a pear flat against a fence or wall, using very little space.

A pear is as trainable as an apple and, where fireblight can be controlled, a trained tree can last 75 years. Plant pears as espaliers, train them to 45-degree angles for an informal hedge, or try them in tubs as a single cordon or on a trellis.

'Clapp's Favorite' pear

Pears bear on long-lived spurs, much as apples do. These spurs last a long time if you're careful not to damage them when picking the fruit.

You don't need to thin fruit, but if a very heavy crop sets, remove fruit that is damaged or very undersized. Thin a few weeks before harvest.

All pears can be considered to need a pollinator. Use almost any other pear. However, 'Bartlett' is a poor pollinator for 'Seckel'.

Most fruits are best when picked ripe, or nearly so. Pears are the exception. A tree-ripe pear breaks down and turns soft and brown at the core. Always harvest pears when they have reached full size but are still green and very firm. Hold them in a cool, dark place if you intend to eat them within a few weeks. For longer storage, refrigerate the harvested fruit, then remove it from cold storage about a week before you want to use it. Pears ripen faster if they are held with other pears in a poorly ventilated spot. For fast ripening, place several in a plastic bag together.

Early midseason cultivars. 'Ayres'. Origin: Tennessee. A cross of 'Garber' and 'Anjou', this fruit is golden russet with a rose tint. The flesh is juicy, sweet, and good for eating fresh or canning. The tree is fireblight resistant. Good for the South. (2)

'Clapp's Favorite'. This large yellow fruit with red cheeks resembles 'Bartlett'. The flesh is soft, sweet, and good both for eating and canning. The tree is attractively shaped and very productive, but highly susceptible to fireblight. Since it is very hardy, the cultivar is best in cold, late-spring zones. Good for the North and West. Widely available.

Below left: A mixed harvest of pears includes tiny 'Old Home'.

Below: Pick the 'Bartlett' pear green (left) and eat it when it begins to yellow (center). The golden pear (right) is overripe.

'Moonglow' pear

'Max-Red Bartlett' pear

French 'Bosc' pear

'Moonglow'. Origin: Maryland. This large, attractive fruit is soft and juicy with a mild flavor. Use it for canning or eating fresh. The tree is very upright and vigorous, heavily spurred, and begins bearing a good crop when quite young. It resists fireblight, so it is good wherever the disease is a severe problem. Good for all zones. Widely available.

'Orient'. Origin: California. This nearly round fruit has firm flesh that makes it a good canner; however, the flavor is too mild for a good fresh pear. The tree produces moderate crops and is resistant to fireblight. Good for the South, from Tennessee. (2, 13D, 17, 35, 38)

Midseason cultivars. 'Bartlett'. This familiar major commercial pear is yellow, medium-to-large, and thin-skinned. The flesh is very sweet and tender, fine for eating, and good for canning as well. The tree does not have especially good form and is subject to fireblight. It takes summer heat, provided there is adequate cold in winter. In cool climates it sets poorly without a pollinator (any variety but 'Seckel'). Good for all zones. Widely available.

'Devoe'. Origin: New York. The long fruit somewhat resembles 'Bosc', but the greenish yellow to yellow color is closer to 'Bartlett'. The tree is vigorous, tolerant of fireblight and pear psylla. Good for the South. (2, 13)

'Douglas'. This cultivar is a hybrid of the sand pear. The smallish fruit is greenish yellow with some acidity. The flesh is tender and contains grit cells. The tree is markedly resistant to fireblight, and although hardy does not need long winter chilling. Good for the South and West. (16, 25)

'Lincoln'. Called by some "the most dependable pear for the Midwest," this cultivar bears large fruits abundantly. The tree is extremely hardy and blight resistant. Good for the North and South. (16)

'Magness'. Origin: Maryland. The medium-size oval fruit has a slight russet color. The flesh is highly perfumed. The tree is vigorous and spreads widely for a pear. This variety needs a pollinator, which can be any other pear. It is highly resistant to fireblight. Good for the South and West. (1, 2D, 4, 12, 13D, 17, 23, 31D, 35)

'Maxine'. ('Starking Delicious'). Origin: Ohio. This large and attractive fruit has firm, juicy, sweet white flesh. The tree is somewhat blight-resistant. Good for the North and South. (12, 16, 26D, 31D)

'Max-Red Bartlett'. Origin: Washington. A bud mutation of 'Bartlett', the fruit is cranberry-red on the tree, changing to bright red when picked. The flesh is finer-grained and sweeter than 'Bartlett'. The tree form resembles 'Bartlett', but the shoots and leaves have the reddish tinge of the fruit. It is susceptible to blight, and in cool climates needs a pollinator—any pear but 'Seckel'. Good for the West. (1, 12, 25D, 26D, 32D, 34)

'Parker'. Origin: Minnesota. This medium-to-large pear is yellow with a red blush. The flesh is white, juicy, and pleasantly sweet. The tree is upright, vigorous, and fairly hardy, but susceptible to fireblight. Good for the North. (11, 21, 28)

Late midseason cultivars. 'Anjou'. A French pear originating in the mild area near the Loire, the fruit is large and green, with a stocky neck. The flesh has a mild flavor and is not especially juicy, but firm. It stores well and is good for eating fresh or canning. The tree is upright and vigorous, but susceptible to fireblight. It is not a tree for hot-summer areas. Good for the North and West. Widely available.

'Bosc'. Origin: France. This long, narrow fruit has a heavy russet color. The flesh is firm, even crisp, with a heavy perfume that makes some people consider it among the very finest pears. It is good fresh or canned, and is fine for cooking. The tree is very large and highly susceptible to fireblight. The fruit does not take cold storage. Good for the North and West. Widely available.

'Duchess'. Origin: France. This pear is greenish yellow and very large. The flesh is buttery, melting, and of fine flavor. The tree is symmetrical and

'Seckel' pear

bears annually. Good for the North. (2, 4, 12D, 16D, 19D, 22D, 24DS, 33D)

'Gorham'. Origin: New York. Of excellent quality, this fruit strongly resembles 'Bartlett', but ripens later and can be stored longer. The tree is dense, upright, vigorous, and productive. Good for the North and South. (27D, 31D)

'Mericourt'. Origin: Tennessee. This pear is green to yellow-green, sometimes blushed deep red and flecked with brown. The creamy-white flesh is nearly grit-free and has a sprightly flavor. Good fresh or for canning. A vigorous tree, it will withstand −23°F. during full dormancy. It resists both fireblight and leaf spot. Good for the South. (31D)

'Patten'. Origin: Louisiana. This large, juicy pear is particularly good fresh, and fair for canning. Since the tree is especially hardy, it should be considered for the northern Mississippi Valley, where 'Bartlett' and 'Anjou' fail. Good for the North. (11)

'Seckel'. This is a small, yellow-brown fruit that is not especially attractive but has the finest aroma and flavor of any home-garden pear. Eat it fresh or use it whole for spiced preserves. The tree is highly productive and very fireblight-resistant. It sets fruit best with a pollinator, any pear but 'Bartlett'. Good for all zones. Widely available.

Late cultivars. 'Comice'. Origin: France. This large, round fruit is green to yellow-green, with a tough skin. Of all pears, this is the finest for eating. It is sweet, aromatic, and juicy, but not for canning. The large, vigorous tree is slow to bear and moderately susceptible to fireblight. It sets fruit better with a pollinator. This is the specialty of the Medford region in Oregon, but does well in home gardens along the California coast. Good for the West. (2, 32D, 33, 34, 37D, 40DS)

'Dumont'. Of European origin, this is a large pear with blushed yellow skin. The flesh is firm and juicy, with a sweet, rich flavor. It is one of the best winter pears. The tree tends to bear in alternate years, especially as it grows old. Good for the North. (27D, 31D)

'Kieffer'. This sand pear hybrid has large yellow fruit that is often gritty and therefore poor for fresh use, but it keeps well in storage and is excellent for cooking and canning. The tree is especially recommended because of a high resistance to fireblight, amounting to near immunity. It needs little winter chill but stands both cold and heat well, so its range is wide. Good for the South and West. Widely available.

The orange-red fruits of the persimmon hang on after the leaves have fallen, to create a display of winter color.

Persimmons

The persimmon belongs to the same family of plants as the ebony tree of southern Asia. The American persimmon, *Diospyros virginiana*, grows as a native from Connecticut to Kansas and then southward, but it won't take the extreme cold of the northern plains or northern New England. It has small edible fruits to 2½ inches in diameter.

The large persimmon found in the market is the Japanese persimmon, *D. kaki*, and its many cultivars. It could be far more popular than it is if more gardeners realized the great value of both tree and fruit. The tree grows well in any well-drained soil and makes a fine medium-size shade tree with large leaves that turn a rich gold in fall. A heavy crop of orange fruit holds on until winter, decorating the bare branches. It can be grown in the southern states and on the West Coast.

Two kinds of fruit exist. The large, pointed kind sold in markets must be fully ripe and very soft before eaten or it is astringent. It is excellent in cooking, adding its spicy flavor to fruit breads, cakes, puddings, and pies; and if you peel and dry it when it's firm-ripe, the flavor is extraordinary. A smaller, flattened fruit is eaten while still firm.

Above left: Oriental persimmon 'Hachiya' in autumn

Above: 'Fuyu' Oriental persimmon

Persimmon foliage is large and glossy, with leaves reaching up to 6 inches in length. The new spring leaves are bronze or reddish, and in fall they turn to shades of yellow, pink, and red. The fruit hangs on into the first frosts and is orange with a red blush. Eat it when it softens, or use it as you would applesauce or bananas. If you want to store it, mash the soft pulp out of the skin for freezing, and discard the tough skin.

Use a persimmon tree as an attractive background plant in a shrub border, or in front of evergreens (where it shows off its leaves and fruit best). Since the persimmon grows slowly, it takes well to espalier training. Train it informally against a flat surface, or use a trellis to form a persimmon hedge. It will also grow well as a single lawn-tree, but you'll have a problem in late fall when the soft fruit drops and squashes.

Fruit is borne on new wood. On a naturally shaped tree it will set on the outer portion.

Persimmons are often allowed to grow naturally, forming globe-shaped trees to 25 or 30 feet high. They can be pruned back in spring to keep them smaller. Little pruning is necessary, however. Train the young tree to 3 widely spaced scaffolds and let it alone thereafter, or control it by cutting each year to strong lateral branches, removing as much growth as you need to maintain the size you want. In pruning an espalier, cut off enough of the previous year's growth to expose the most interesting lines of the plant.

Thinning fruit is unnecessary but will help to keep lawn trees neater.

American persimmons are normally dioecious, meaning that some trees are male, producing pollen but no fruit, while others are female. You will need a female tree for fruit, and a male close by. Plant both unless you have wild trees near your garden. An occasional improved cultivar has fruit crops without requiring a separate pollinator, but these are still not generally available.

Most Japanese persimmons set fruit without a separate pollinator, but some are self-sterile, so check your cultivar selections carefully. Oriental persimmons also stand winter temperatures to about zero degrees F., but they need only a short period of chill to fruit well.

In the West, the persimmon has no serious pests. In the East, a flat-headed borer may attack the trunk and can be removed by hand.

Cultivars. *American persimmons.* These are available from the following catalog sources: 4, 12, 14, 16, 35. Good varieties to look for include 'Early Golden', 'Garretson', 'Hicks', 'John Rick', and 'Juhl'.

Oriental persimmons. These are available from the following sources: 6, 14, 35, 37, 38, 46. Good varieties include 'Chocolate', 'Hachiya', 'Fuyu', 'Tamopan', and 'Tanenashi'.

'Italian Prune' (also called 'Fellenberg') is a typical European plum.

Plums

Of all the stone fruits, plums are the most varied. They range from hardy little cherry plums and sand cherries, to hybrids with the hardiness of natives, to European-type plums. In the milder regions, particularly along the Eastern seaboard, some Japanese-type plums are also grown. Plums bear for 10 to 15 years and sometimes more.

Standard plum trees take space. Expect your tree to fill an area 20 by 20 feet. Bush and cherry plums can be used in smaller spaces and reach 6 feet or so, but may spread as wide or wider. A dwarfed European plum on Nanking cherry roots will reach 10 or 12 feet in height.

Plums bear on spurs along the older branches, with the heaviest production on wood that is from 2 to 4 years old.

Check the cultivar list for pollinators. Most plums need a pollinator, although European kinds are generally partly or entirely self-fertile.

Plums need little or no thinning except for the large-fruited Japanese kinds. The young trees should be trained as discussed on page 72. Bush varieties need their oldest shoots trimmed off at ground level after about 4 years of bearing to encourage new growth.

Japanese plums overgrow and overbear. Cut back the long whips as discussed under "Apricots," and thin fruit at thumbnail size, leaving 4 to 6 inches between remaining fruits.

Tree plums don't lend themselves to confinement, so use bush types if your space is limited. Use bush types also as shrubby screens or try them in containers.

Brown rot is a major concern and means summer spraying (pages 49–55).

European plums. These plums tend to be small, and most varieties are egg-shaped. The flesh is rather dry and very sweet. Prunes are the sweetest and easiest to dry. The plants are fairly hardy but also do well where winter is mild. All cultivars are self-pollinating, except for those noted.

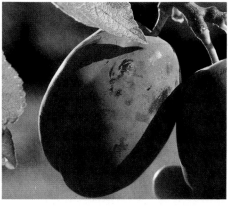

Early cultivar. 'Earliblue'. This blue plum has tender, green-yellow flesh resembling 'Stanley', but softer. The tree is hardy but bears late. Production is moderate, but fine for the home garden. Use 'Mohawk' as a pollinator. It is best planted in the North, and ripens in mid- to late July in Michigan. (33, 41)

Midseason cultivars. 'Damson'. This old plum from Europe is derived from a different species than other European plums. The smallish blue fruits are best for jam, jelly, and preserves. Improved varieties include 'Blue Damson', 'French Damson', and 'Shropshire Damson'. The trees are small and self-pollinating, and fruit ripens at the end of August or in September. It is a late plum in the North. Good for all zones. Widely available.

'Green Gage' ('Reine Claude'). This is an old European cultivar. Greenish yellow fruit has amber flesh and is good fresh, cooked, or preserved. Trees are medium-size and self-pollinating. Fruit ripens in mid-July, later in the North. Good for all zones. Widely available.

'Stanley'. Origin: New York. The most widely planted European plum in the East, Midwest, and South, this tree has large, dark blue fruit with firm, richly flavored yellow flesh. It bears heavily every year, is hardy into central Iowa, and is self-pollinating. Fruit ripens after mid-August, into September in northern regions. Good for the North. Widely available.

'Sugar'. This very sweet, dark blue plum is fairly large and excellent for home drying and canning. The trees are self-pollinating and bear in alternate years, with light crops in off years. Fruit ripens after July 15. Good for all zones. (45)

'Yellow Egg'. This golden yellow plum has a thick skin and yellow flesh. The round-topped, vigorous tree is hardy and productive. In the West the tree is planted in Washington. It is self-pollinating and fruit ripens in late August. Good for the North and West. (2, 34)

Late cultivars. 'Bluefre'. This large blue freestone has yellow flesh. The trees are vigorous, self-pollinating, and bear young. Fruit hangs on well after ripening. It has some sensitivity to brown rot. Fruit ripens early September. Good for the North. (7, 33, 41DS)

'French Prune'. The small fruit is red to purplish black and very sweet with a mild flavor. This is the main prune variety in California. The tree is large and long-lived, often surviving even after orchards have become housing developments. It is self-pollinating, and fruit ripens in late August to September. Good for the South and West. Widely available in California.

'Italian Prune' ('Fellenberg'). This dark blue plum is very sweet and good for dessert, canning, or drying. It has been the major plum of the Washington–Oregon areas. Fruit ripens in late August and September. Good for the South and West. Widely available.

'President'. This large, dark blue fruit has amber flesh and ripens very late, after other plums. It lacks outstanding flavor, but use it for winter cooking or canning. Use another late European plum as a pollinator. Fruit ripens in Michigan at the end of September. Good for the North. (1, 14, 34, 41DS)

Above left: Plum blossoms add a delicate beauty to the landscape in spring.

Above center: Blue is the most common color for the European plum.

Above: 'Green Gage' (also called 'Reine Claude') plum

'Stanley' plum

'Yellow Egg' plum

Japanese (Oriental) plums. The fruit is relatively large, soft, and juicy. The plants are the least hardy of the various kinds of plum, although selected cultivars are grown in the milder northern regions. Taste before harvest. All cultivars are self-pollinating, except for those noted.

Early cultivars. 'Beauty'. Origin: California. This medium-to-large plum is bright red, with amber flesh tinged red. Use it fresh or cooked. The tree is strong and vigorous. It is self-pollinating, but use 'Santa Rosa' for better pollination. Fruit ripens in early June in California. Good for all zones. (4D, 41DS)

'Bruce'. Origin: Texas. This large plum has red skin, red flesh, and good flavor. The fruit matures early. The tree bears young and heavily. Use 'Santa Rosa' as a pollinator. Fruit ripens in June. Good for the North and West. (13)

'Early Golden'. Origin: Canada. This medium-size, round plum is yellow and of fair quality. The stone is small and free. The tree is very vigorous, outgrowing other varieties, but it has a tendency to bear in alternate years. Thin carefully. Pollinate with 'Shiro' or 'Burbank'. Fruit ripens in Michigan in mid-July. Good for the North. (27, 38)

'Santa Rosa'. Origin: California. This widely popular large plum has deep crimson skin and flesh that is purplish near the skin, and yellow streaked with pink near the pit. It is good for dessert or canning. It is self-pollinating, or use any early or midseason plum for improved pollination. Fruit ripens in California in mid-June, later in the North. Good for all zones. Widely available.

Early midseason cultivars. 'Abundance'. Origin: California. This plum is red-purple with yellow flesh, tender, and softens quickly. It is good for dessert or cooking. The tree tends strongly to bear every other year. Use 'Methley' or 'Shiro' as a pollinator. Fruit ripens in Michigan in late July. Good for the North. (4D, 6D, 24DS, 35D, 41DS)

'Methley'. This small-to-medium fruit is reddish purple with red flesh and excellent flavor. It ripens over a long period, needing several pickings. The tree is upright, with hardy flower buds. It is self-pollinating, but for better crops use 'Shiro' or 'Burbank'. Fruit ripens in Michigan in mid-July, earlier in the South. Good for the North. Widely available.

'Satsuma'. This is a blood plum with red juice. The meaty fruit is small to medium, with a dull, dark red skin, red flesh, and a small pit. The flavor is mild and good. Use it for dessert or preserves. Use 'Santa Rosa' or 'Wickson' as a pollinator. Good for all zones. Widely available.

'Shiro'. This medium-to-large plum is round, yellow, and of good flavor. The tree produces heavily. Use it fresh or for cooking. Use 'Early Golden', 'Methley', or 'Santa Rosa' as a pollinator. Fruit ripens in early July in California and the South, in late July in Michigan. Good for all zones. Widely available.

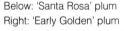

Below: 'Santa Rosa' plum
Right: 'Early Golden' plum

Midseason cultivars. 'Burbank'. Origin: California. This large red plum has amber flesh of excellent flavor. The trees are fairly small and somewhat drooping. Use the fruit for canning or dessert. Use 'Early Golden' or 'Santa Rosa' as a pollinator. Fruit ripens in early August in the Northwest, in mid-July in California. Good for all zones. Widely available.

'Duarte'. Origin: California. The medium-large, dull red fruit has silvery markings. The flesh is deep red. Fruit keeps well and is tart when cooked. Use 'Santa Rosa' or 'Satsuma' as a pollinator. Fruit ripens in late July. Good for all zones. (7, 34D)

'Howard Miracle'. Origin: California. The fruit is yellow with a heavy red blush when ripe. The flesh is yellow and rather acid, with a distinctive, very good flavor, reminiscent of pineapple. The tree is self-pollinating and very vigorous. Fruit ripens after July 15. Good for all zones. (42D)

'Ozark Premier'. Origin: Missouri. This extremely large red plum has yellow flesh. The trees are self-pollinating, hardy, and productive. Fruit ripens early in August. Good for the North and South. Widely available.

Late cultivar. 'Elephant Heart'. Origin: California. This large, thick-skinned fruit is mottled purple and green. The flesh is blood red. Trees are strong and hardy. Fruit ripens over a long period. Use 'Santa Rosa' as a pollinator. Fruit ripens in late July or August. Good for all zones. (10, 14, 31, 33)

Hardy plums. These plums were especially selected and bred for the coldest northern and Great Plains climates.

'Pipestone'. Origin: Minnesota. This large red fruit has tough skin that is easy to peel. The flesh is yellow and of excellent quality but somewhat stringy. The tree is vigorous and hardy, of reliable performance in cold regions. Use 'Toka' or 'Superior' as a pollinator. (11, 19, 21, 28, 41DS)

'Superior'. Origin: Minnesota. This large, conical red fruit with russet dots and heavy bloom has yellow, firm flesh excellent for eating fresh. The tree bears very young and prolifically. Use 'Toka' as a pollinator. (11, 12D, 16D, 19D, 22, 25D, 26, 28)

'Toka'. Origin: Minnesota. This large, pointed fruit is medium red, and often described as apricot-colored. The flesh is firm and yellow, with a rich, spicy flavor. The tree is a heavy producer, spreading, and medium-size, but may be short-lived. Use 'Superior' as a pollinator. (11, 19, 41)

'Underwood'. Origin: Minnesota. This very large, red, freestone plum has golden yellow flesh that is somewhat stringy but of good dessert quality. Ripening extends over a long season from July. The tree is vigorous and among the most hardy. Use 'Superior' as a pollinator. (11, 12, 16, 28, 33)

'Waneta'. Origin: South Dakota. This is a large, reddish purple plum with yellow flesh. Use 'Superior' as a pollinator. (12, 16)

Above left: Oriental plums are larger and juicier, and they tend to red tones.
Above: 'Burbank' plum

'Wonderful' fruiting pomegranate

Pomegranates

With its shiny leaves, flashy orange flowers, and bright red fruit, the pomegranate is one of the most beautiful fruiting plants. The young leaves have a reddish tint in spring and are bright yellow in fall, providing a background that makes the fruits especially attractive.

Pomegranates are often thought of as a tropical or desert fruit, but in fact they withstand winter temperatures down to about 10°F. While they do ripen their fruit best in very hot, arid climates, you can still harvest edible fruit in cooler areas. They are ideal plants for the desert Southwest because they also stand considerable drought.

Many people who admire the pomegranate as an ornamental shrub or tree seem to have trouble eating it. The edible portion is the juicy scarlet flesh around the abundant seeds. If you score the skin just down to these seeds in about six places, cutting from stem to flower, you can open the fruit and expose all the seeds at once. They are good in fruit salads and make an excellent syrup when cooked with sugar and a little water. This syrup is sold commercially as grenadine.

You can grow pomegranates as fountain-shaped shrubs or as single- or multiple-trunked trees. They reach about 10 to 12 feet tall under ideal conditions, but often remain smaller. A shrub can spread to 6 or 8 feet across. Since they fruit on new growth, you can prune them back heavily without loss of flowers or fruit.

Blossoms form on the current year's growth, and as the fruit grows heavier, it pulls down the slender new branches, making a decorative weeping effect. Although the plant will stand drought, the fruit will split if a tree is allowed to dry out completely and is then watered. For a good crop, keep the moisture level even.

You can prune as you like to shape the plants, but no pruning is necessary if you choose to let it grow naturally.

Thinning is not necessary. An excess crop is very decorative if left on the tree. The trees are self-fertile, so even a single specimen will bear fruit.

Normally pomegranates have no pest or disease problems, but leaves can develop fungus diseases in humid climates.

Cultivar. The variety 'Wonderful' is the only fruiting pomegranate you're likely to see in the nursery.

Below: Pomegranate fruit grows to three times this size and turns bright red.

Right: Flashy orange pomegranate flowers last for weeks.

BERRIES

A little sunlight and a pot is all you need to grow luscious breakfast strawberries, and many of the other berries offer rich rewards for small investments of time and space.

The small-fruited plants can return bumper crops with only minimum effort, and several of the shrubby or vining plants can also add beauty to the ornamental landscape.

In considering berries, space and the number of plants needed for a reasonable supply of fruit are factors to be worked out. If the plants are right for your climate and are given excellent care, the number of plants necessary to supply a family of five would go something like this:

- ☐ Strawberries: 25 (20–30 quarts)
- ☐ Raspberries: 24 (20–30 quarts)
- ☐ Blackberries: 12 (9–15 quarts)
- ☐ Blueberries: 6 (9–15 quarts)
- ☐ Currants: 2 (6–12 quarts)
- ☐ Gooseberries: 2 (6–12 quarts)

Strawberries are without question the easiest to work into any space you may have available. Even on a south-facing apartment terrace you can produce a crop in containers such as strawberry jars or a moss-lined wire strawberry tree. An ideal plant for containers, where you can find it, is the European wild strawberry, or *fraise des bois*. This plant won't make runners. It grows in a clump, so a container planting stays compact.

The cane berries—blackberries and raspberries—take more space, although you can grow a few in large containers. If you train them carefully along a fence or trellis and keep them pruned, they won't take very much space; but they will produce heavy crops of fruit that you just can't buy, since the finest flavor disappears during the transportation and holding time needed to get them to your grocery store.

Blueberries, currants, and gooseberries make extremely ornamental shrubs, covered with bloom in spring, and with decorative fruit in later seasons. Blueberries require light, acid soil and constant moisture, so try them where you would grow azaleas. Currants and gooseberries are an interim host to a serious disease of five-needle pines, so in some areas you're not allowed to plant them. Where they are permitted, nothing takes less care, is more decorative, or gives a more useful crop.

Grapes, of course, are among the best landscaping plants, with lush foliage, fall color, and interesting vines. Use them on arbors, against walls, as fences, or as freestanding shrubs on a pole or trellis. Choose varieties recommended for your climate, since grapes are especially sensitive to heat.

Even the smallest garden has room for a clump of strawberries.

Blackberries and Raspberries

Blackberries. Blackberries and raspberries are closely related and have similar growing requirements, but blackberries are larger, more vigorous, and some cultivars are less hardy. Blackberries come in two fairly distinct forms—erect and trailing—and have a number of different names.

The blackberry of ordinary conversation is a stiff-caned, fairly hardy plant that can stand by itself if properly pruned. The trailing kind is generally called a *dewberry*, and it is tender and grown mainly in the South. In addition, trailing plants from the Pacific Coast are sold under their cultivar names; for example, 'Boysen' and 'Logan'. These will freeze without winter protection.

Blackberries like a light, well-drained soil with high moisture-holding capacity. It is important not to plant them where tomatoes, potatoes, or eggplant have grown previously, since the site may be infected with verticillium wilt and the berries cannot grow there.

Top: 'Olallie' blackberries grow on a neat wooden frame.

Above: 'Olallie' is a low-chill variety.

Plant in early spring a month before the last frost. Set plants 4 to 6 feet apart in rows 6 to 9 feet apart. Before planting, clip canes to 6-inch stubs and plant at the depth they grew in the nursery. As soon as new growth begins, cut any stubs that are left and burn them to protect plants from anthracnose, especially in the South. Several inches of mulch will help keep soil moist, prevent weed growth, and help prevent suckers. Mulches such as fresh straw or sawdust will require added nitrogen. Use any high-nitrogen fertilizer at the rate of $\frac{1}{2}$ to 1 pound per 100 square feet. Don't fertilize too heavily or you'll get lush plant growth at the expense of a fruit crop.

Blackberries fruit on twiggy side branches growing on canes of the previous season. The canes fruit only once and must be removed every year.

See pages 67–72 for pruning and training methods. The stiff-caned berries need no support, but can be confined between two wires to cut back on space. Dewberries should be cut to the ground after fruiting, and burned. The new growth of the last part of summer will fruit the following year, and burning reduces the chances for disease. Keep suckers pulled between rows.

If you disturb or cut roots of blackberries they will sucker badly. If you want more plants, chop off pieces of root beside the parent plants and set them in the new planting site like seed. If you don't want more plants, mulch the planting instead of cultivating for weed control. Blackberries can be more troublesome than any other cultivated plant and, if abandoned, can quickly grow out of control.

Blackberries are subject to enormous numbers of pests and disease. Save yourself trouble by buying certified plants and keeping them away from any wild plants. Some cultivars resist some diseases. Spray for blackberry mite, and don't worry too much about the rest.

Our cultivar list is divided into varieties for the South, the North, and the West, with the South and North separated into erect and trailing berries. Some cultivars are recommended for more than one area of the country, in which case you will be referred to the main entry.

Cultivars for the South. In much of the South, either dewberries or erect blackberries can be planted. In the warmest areas of zone 3, dewberries are probably superior, although there are low-chill blackberries that do well. In zones 5 and 6 choose only the erect blackberry, or be prepared to offer winter protection by burying canes under 2 inches of soil after the first frost, and then digging them out just as buds begin to swell.

Erect blackberries. 'Brainerd'. Origin: Georgia. This large, high-quality fruit is excellent for processing. The plant is productive, vigorous, and very hardy. Locally available.

'Brazos'. This is a popular variety in Texas, Arkansas, and Louisiana. The large fruit matures early and bears over a long period. The plant is vigorous and somewhat resistant to disease. Locally available.

'Ebony King' blackberry

'Darrow'. This hardy, heavy producer ripens in August from canes grown at the end of the previous summer. Fruit is large, glossy black, and of good quality. Widely available.

'Ebony King'. Origin: Michigan. The large fruit is glossy black, sweet, and tangy. It ripens early and resists orange rust. Widely available.

'Eldorado'. This very hardy and productive old variety resembles 'Ebony King' and is totally immune to orange rust. (13)

'Flint'. Origin: Georgia. This blackberry needs only moderate winter chill. The berries are fairly large in clusters of 8 to 15, and the plant is highly resistant to leaf spot and anthracnose. Locally available.

'Humble'. This low-chill Texas variety has large, somewhat soft berries and comparatively few thorns. Locally available.

'Ranger'. This large, firm berry is best only when fully ripe. It is especially recommended for Virginia and similar climates. (2, 13)

'Smoothstem'. Origin: Maryland. The berries ripen late and are rather soft. Production is quite heavy in large clusters. The plant is thornless and hardy from Maryland, southward. (13, 16, 30)

'Williams'. Origin: North Carolina. The medium-size fruits ripen in late June and are very good fresh. The bush is semierect, very vigorous, and thorny. It resists most cane and leaf diseases. Locally available.

Trailing blackberries (dewberries). 'Boysen' ('Nectar'). A Pacific Coast variety with large and aromatic fruit produced over a long season, this plant is vigorous and fairly thorny. (2, 4, 5, 13)

'Carolina'. Origin: North Carolina. The plant is vigorous and productive, with very large berries. It resists septoria leaf spot. Locally available.

'Early June'. Origin: Georgia. The large, round fruit is medium-firm, of excellent flavor, and acid enough for jam, jelly, and pies. Fruit ripens in early June. The plant is semithornless and somewhat resistant to anthracnose and leaf spot. Locally available.

'Flordagrand'. Origin: Florida. The large fruit is very soft and tart, good for cooking and preserves. It ripens very early. Canes are evergreen. It must be planted with 'Oklawaha' for pollination. Locally available.

'Lavaca'. A seedling of 'Boysen' that is hardier than the parent and more resistant to disease, this fruit is firmer and less acid. Locally available.

'Lucretia'. Origin: North Carolina. This hardy old favorite is vigorous and productive with very large, long, soft berries that ripen early. It needs winter protection in the North. (12, 13, 16)

'Oklawaha'. Origin: Florida. This plant resembles 'Flordagrand' and should be planted with it for pollination. Locally available.

'Young'. Origin: Louisiana. Large, purplish-black fruit of excellent flavor is easy to pick. The plant produces few very long canes. Anthracnose is a serious threat. (11, 12, 13, 16, 36)

Cultivars for the North. The trailing berries are really too tender to grow in the North without special protection, but the fruit tends to be more flavorful than the erect kinds. Erect blackberries are not recommended for zones 7 and 8, but will grow elsewhere, and may possibly succeed in the North if you bundle the canes in straw and burlap for the winter.

Erect blackberries. 'Alfred'. Origin: Michigan. This plant produces large, firm berries early. Locally available.

'Bailey'. Origin: New York. The fruit is large, medium firm, and of good quality. The bush is reliably productive. (12, 19)

'Darrow'. See "Cultivars for the South."

'Eldorado'. See "Cultivars for the South."

'Ebony King'. See "Cultivars for the South."

'Hedrick'. Origin: New York. The fruit is large, medium firm, and tart. The bush is reliably productive. Locally available.

'Raven'. Origin: Maryland. This large berry is of high quality fresh or processed. The plant is erect, vigorous, and productive, but rather tender. (2, 13)

'Smoothstem'. See "Cultivars for the South."

'Thornfree'. Origin: Maryland. The medium-large fruit is tart and good. The semi-upright canes reach 8 feet, with up to 30 berries on each fruiting twig. The plant is rather tender. Widely available.

Trailing berries. All are tender and need protection from cold.

'Lucretia'. See "Cultivars for the South."

'Thornless Boysen'. This summer-bearing Pacific Coast berry is flavorful with a fine aroma, and grows on tender plants that must be trained. Bury the canes for the winter. Widely available.

'Thornless Logan'. This Pacific Coast berry is acid, good for jam, pies, and for a syrup base for drinks. Bury the canes in winter. (13, 16)

Cultivars for the West. The lists of cultivars in this section have been divided into three groups: the Pacific Northwest, the interior, and California. There is a considerable amount of overlap among the three groups.

Berries for the Pacific Northwest like mild winters and cool summers. If you try them elsewhere, the climate should approach that mix, as it does along the Northern California coast. California berries need a bit more summer heat and even milder winters. Berries for the interior are of a different kind, with stiff canes. They are hardier in cold winters.

These varieties are not limited only to the region indicated, but they do well there. You will have more success with them if your climate resembles the one indicated.

Below: A woven trellis gives good support for trailing berries.

Right: 'Marion' blackberry

Pacific Northwest. This heading refers to the mild coastal climates, not to the colder eastern areas.

'Aurora'. This very early fruit is large, firm, and of excellent flavor. The canes are pliable and easy to train, and are most productive on the bottom 5 feet, so they do well planted closely and cut back heavily. Locally available.

'Boysen' ('Nectar'). See "Cultivars for the South."

'Cascade'. The flavor of this berry is unsurpassed, fresh or preserved. The plant is vigorous and productive, but tender. (3, 7, 36, 40)

'Marion'. The fruit of this midseason variety is medium to large, long, and of very good flavor. The plants send out a few vigorous canes that are up to 20 feet long and very thorny. (3, 7, 14, 32, 36, 40)

'Thornless Evergreen'. A top commercial berry in Oregon, this variety offers fruit that is large, firm, and sweet. Plants are vigorous and produce heavily, but are very tender. Pinching canes at 24 inches encourages more canes and laterals, and may increase productivity. There is a thorny form. (3, 14, 32, 36, 40)

'Thornless Logan'. This large, reddish, acid berry is best in pies or preserves. It is adapted to the Columbia River area of Washington, the Willamette Valley, and the central coast of California. There is a thorny form. (3, 5, 13, 14, 16, 32, 36)

The interior. The following will grow in eastern Washington, and wherever cold is not too intense. They are stiff-caned, from rigid to somewhat trailing.

'Bailey'. See "Cultivars for the North."

'Darrow'. Origin: New York. The berries are very large and irregular, with firm flesh. They ripen over a very long season, sometimes into fall. The bush is very hardy and reliable. (2, 6, 20)

'Ebony King'. See "Cultivars for the South."

'Smoothstem'. See "Cultivars for the South."

California. The cool north coast suits the Northwest berries, too. Mountain and high-desert gardeners may need berries from the interior list.

'Boysen' ('Nectar'). See "Cultivars for the South." In California, this variety provides an early crop from May 20 to June 20, depending upon the area, and a second crop may extend the harvest through August. It is especially recommended for the Central Coast, Central Valley, and South Coast. Widely available.

'Himalaya'. This late berry is grown in limited quantities in Northern California. Locally available.

'Ollalie'. Origin: Oregon. This is the prime California variety, with large, high-quality berries that are shiny black, firm, and sweet. The canes are thorny and very productive. The plant is a low-chill variety and resists verticillium wilt and mildew. It is especially good for Southern California. (14)

'Young'. See "Cultivars for the South." This one does especially well in Southern California.

Above left: A double-wire trellis provides support for a large number of trailing berries woven along the wires.

Above center: Make the crossbar sturdy to hold the weight of the canes as they leaf out.

Above: The lowest wires support growing canes.

Below: This trellis also acts as a support for netting to protect the berry crop from birds.

Raspberries. Raspberries are the hardiest of the cane berries, and perhaps the most worthwhile home-garden crop for several reasons. First, prices for the market fruit are high, since care and labor are expensive. Then too, market raspberries may be subject to a long holding and handling period so that fruit loses its finest flavor and may be bruised. Home-garden fruit can be picked and eaten at its peak.

The thing that makes a raspberry a raspberry is the fact that it pulls free of its core when you pick it. Other bramble fruits take the core with them. The red raspberry is the most popular, but they come in a variety of colors and plant forms—yellow, purple, and black fruits, with the reds and yellows growing on trailing plants and the purple and black fruits growing on stiff plants. Do not try both red and black raspberries in the same garden. Reds sometimes carry a virus that they can tolerate, but which is fatal to blacks. Virus-free stock will spare you this trouble.

Unfortunately for southern gardeners, raspberries do poorly in much of the South. They need cold winters and a long, cool spring. Everbearing plants don't like any high heat. They can be grown by gardeners in zones 5 and 6, and perhaps a few high-ground gardeners in zone 4 who are willing to take some failures.

California and Arizona gardeners are similarly unfortunate. Raspberries do not like spring and summer heat, so only the red varieties will grow, and they are recommended only for coastal or mountain regions. The prime berry country in the coastal states is western Washington around Puget Sound (zone 8b), and the Willamette Valley of Oregon. Good berries grow through zones 7, but may need winter protection in the coldest areas.

Wherever you grow them, cut the nursery plants to 6- to 12-inch stubs and plant them about 2 to 4 feet apart and 2 inches deeper than they grew in the nursery row. Your rows should be 6 or 7 feet apart.

On most raspberries, the fruit forms on side shoots, along canes that grew the previous year. One group of red or yellow raspberries produces some fruit at the top of current-season canes in fall, then produces a second crop on the rest of the cane the following year.

New canes should be laid carefully along the rows until it's time to prune away old canes, then lifted and trained. Pull out suckers of red raspberries that sprout between the rows.

Raspberries are subject to all the same troubles as dewberries, but in the cold climates where raspberries will grow you'll have less trouble. Verticillium in the soil rules them out entirely. Black raspberries are susceptible to virus diseases and should be planted at least 700 feet from any reds.

If you want to enlarge a planting, it is important to know the difference between black and red raspberries. Blacks and purples arch their canes to the ground and root at the top to form new plants. If you want more, leave a few canes unpruned and in late summer pin the tip to the ground. Throw on a little soil if you like. Then dig and separate the new plant in spring.

Red raspberries send up root suckers. You can dig and replant them just before growth begins. Take a piece of root and cut back the top.

Raspberries are extremely hardy, so no special protection is needed except in the coldest mountain and Plains climates. Where winter temperatures stay extremely low for long periods, you should protect your plants.

Lay canes of the current season along the row or trellis, pinning portions that arch upward. Be careful not to snap them. Where mice are not likely to be a problem, cover the canes with straw or sawdust to a depth of several inches, and then cover the mulch with poultry netting to hold it in place. If you know that mouse damage is probable in winter, bury the canes in earth about 2 inches deep.

In spring, uncover the canes before they begin to leaf out, just as the buds swell. If the buds break while still covered, they will be extremely tender to even light frost.

Single-crop and everbearing raspberries may be red or yellow. They require trellising.

Red or yellow cultivars

Single-crop. All fruit is borne on laterals that sprout from the year-old canes. Crops come in late spring or early summer.

'Amber'. This yellow berry is an excellent dessert fruit. Good for the North. (2)

'Canby'. These large, firm, midseason berries are good for freezing. The plants are semithornless and do best in light soils in the Northwest. Good for the West. (3, 13, 16)

'Cuthbert'. Once the leading commercial raspberry, and still unexcelled for dessert, canning, or freezing, this variety is low-yielding and difficult to pick, which are not problems in the home garden. Good for the West. Locally available.

'Fairview'. These berries are large to fairly large and light red. The tall, branched canes are moderately hardy. It is especially suited to western Washington, and generally good for the West.

'Hilton'. This berry is the largest of all reds, very attractive, and of excellent quality. Plants are vigorous, productive, and hardy. Good for the North. (3, 13, 40)

'Latham'. This early midseason variety is the standard eastern red raspberry. The berry is large, firm, and attractive, with a tart flavor. Plants somewhat resist virus disease. Good for the South and West. Widely available.

'Newburgh'. Often spelled 'Newberg', this productive midseason red variety yields large, firm berries. Good for the North and West. (3, 7, 16, 22, 24, 27, 30)

'New Washington'. This is an excellent coastal variety grown in California. The late-ripening berries are deep red, moderately firm, and sweet. Also good for the South. Locally available.

'Pocahontas'. This recent introduction has large, firm, medium-red berries with a tart flavor. The plant is winter hardy and productive. Good for the South. (2)

'Puyallup'. These late-ripening large berries are somewhat soft. The plant does best in light soils in the Northwest, and is generally good for the West. Locally available.

'Summer'. This medium-to-large berry is firm and sweet, with intense

Above left: Blackcap raspberries produce abundantly on erect plants.
Above: Blackcaps ready to pick.
Below: 'Latham' red raspberry

The core stays on the plant when a raspberry is picked.

'Heritage' everbearing raspberry

flavor. Some strains crumble badly. The plants do well in heavy soil and are recommended for western Washington or along the coast to California. Locally available.

'Sunrise'. This early variety offers firm, fine-textured fruit of good quality. The plant is hardy and very tolerant of anthracnose, leaf spot, and cane blight. Good for the South. (4, 35)

'Taylor'. This variety offers mid-to-late, firm red berries of excellent quality. Plants are vigorous and hardy. Good for the North. Locally available.

'Willamette'. The berries ripen in midseason, are large, round, firm, and good for freezing or canning. This is a vigorous, widely planted commercial variety. Good for the West. (3, 13, 34, 40)

Everbearing (summer-and-fall-bearing). Everbearing raspberries produce a crop in fall at the end of new canes, and then another in early summer of the following year. In California, the second crop may succumb to heat prostration. In the Northwest, these may produce a little fruit throughout the spring and summer.

'Cherokee'. The berries are large and firm. The plant is winter-hardy and productive. Good for the South, but particularly for the Piedmont area of Virginia. (2)

'Durham'. These berries have very good flavor. The plants are very hardy and productive, bearing a second crop early. Good for the North. (4, 13, 25)

'Fallgold'. Golden yellow berries distinguish this plant. Good for the North. Widely available.

'Fallred'. The berries are of fair quality, but often crumbly. The plants are nearly thornless. The first crop appears in spring. Good for the South and North. Widely available.

'Heritage'. Medium-size, firm fruit ripens in July and September. The plants are vigorous, stiff-caned, and need little support. Mow all the canes in late winter to get a single August crop and save pruning. Good for all zones. Widely available.

'Indian Summer'. This fruit is large and of good quality. The first crop is light, the fall crop very late and abundant. Good for all zones. (3, 4, 6, 13, 16, 34, 40)

'Ranere' ('St. Regis'). This variety has small, bright red berries of only fair quality, but provides a second crop, except in the warmest areas. Good for the West. Locally available.

'September'. These medium-to-large berries are of good quality. The plant is vigorous and hardy—one of the best in coldest regions. Good for the North and South. (5, 13, 16, 19, 24, 32, 35)

'Southland'. Recommended for farther south than any other, this berry was developed in North Carolina, but is not recommended for the coastal plain. It is a large fruit of fair quality. Good for the South. (2, 33, 43)

Purple cultivars. Plants are tall and stiff and bear a single crop.

'Amethyst'.This early berry is a good-quality introduction from Iowa. Good for the North. (8, 12, 19)

'Clyde'. This early berry is large, firm, dark purple, and of excellent quality. The plant is vigorous. Good for the North. (13, 26)

'Sodus'. This midseason berry is large, firm, and of good quality, but tart. Plants are productive. Good for the North. (11, 12, 13, 16, 19)

Black (blackcap) cultivars. Gardeners in the South and West should be aware that black raspberries are least well able to tolerate mild climates. They need cold, and do poorly in western Washington, although they are planted in the Willamette Valley and elsewhere in Oregon. They bear a single crop on 1-year-old canes.

'Allen'. This variety provides large, attractive berries on a vigorous and productive plant. Good for the North. (2, 13, 21, 22, 26)

'Black Hawk'. This late variety bears large berries of good flavor and yield. Good for the North. Widely available.

'Black Hawk' black raspberry

'Bristol'. These attractive, glossy black berries are large, firm, and of good quality. They must be fully ripe or you can't pick them. Good for the South and West. Widely available.

'Cumberland'. This favored variety has large, firm berries of fine flavor. Plants are vigorous and productive. Good for the South and North. Widely available.

'Logan' ('New Logan'). This variety produces heavy crops of large, glossy, good-quality berries. Plants hold up in drought and tolerate mosaic and other raspberry diseases. Good for the South and North. (2, 4, 11, 13, 40)

'Manteo'. Origin: North Carolina. The fruit resembles 'Cumberland' but the plant survives farther south than any other. Good for the South. Locally available.

'Morrison'. This variety bears later than others listed here. The berries are large, but the crop may be light. Good for the South and West. (12, 19, 25)

'Munger'. The medium-size fruit is of good quality. The plants are especially recommended for western Oregon. They are worth trying in western Washington, but may succumb to disease. Good for the West. (3, 40)

Blueberries

Blueberries demand the right climate and planting soil, but take very little care if you provide suitable conditions. They are about as hardy as a peach, but need a fair amount of winter chill, and will not grow well in mild-winter climates.

Blueberries belong to the heath family, and count azaleas, rhododendrons, mountain-laurel (*Kalmia*), and huckleberries among their cousins. If any of these grow naturally near your garden, or if you have prepared an artificial site that suits them, then blueberries will also do well.

Blueberries like soil rich in organic material such as peat—very acid, but extremely well drained. Soils such as these are usual in areas of high rainfall, which is lucky, since the berries need constant moisture, even though they cannot tolerate standing water.

There are major commercial plantings of blueberries in New Jersey, especially Burlington and Atlantic Counties; in Michigan, in certain areas of the Lower Peninsula; in Washington and Oregon; and to a certain extent in New York, Massachusetts, and Indiana.

Southern gardeners have a choice of two kinds of blueberries, depending on climate. The high-bush blueberry grows commercially in large plantings in southeastern and western North Carolina. A home gardener who hopes to succeed with the plant should live in, or north of, that area. If you know of native blueberries near your home, nursery plants should do well.

The rabbiteye blueberry, or southern high-bush blueberry, grows wild along streambeds in Georgia and northern Florida. With proper care it thrives where muscadine grapes succeed.

Soil must be extremely well drained and acid. You must plant in raised areas if there is any chance of water standing around the roots for a day or more. For both drainage and acidification, add large amounts of peat moss or other organic material to the planting soil, up to three-quarters peat moss by volume for soils that tend to be heavy. Never add manure; it is alkaline. Second, dig a planting hole somewhat broader and deeper than the roots of the young plant. Never cramp the roots into a small hole. Spread the roots in the hole and press soil firmly over them.

Set high-bush blueberry plants about 4 feet apart. Choose two varieties for cross-pollination. Since the rabbiteye plants grow much larger, you can set them up to 8 feet apart, although they can also be set closer and blended into each other.

Do not feed plants the first year. In succeeding years, use cottonseed meal, ammonium sulfate, or any product suitable for camellias, azaleas, or rhododendrons.

'Dixi' high-bush blueberries produce generous clusters of large berries.

'Earliblue' blueberry

'Northland' blueberry

Blueberries require constant light moisture in the soil, and cultivating damages their shallow roots. For both these reasons, you should mulch the plants heavily. Use any organic material such as straw, leaves, peat moss, or a combination, and renew it regularly to keep it about 6 inches deep. Some materials will use nitrogen as they decay, so you will have to compensate with extra feeding.

Pruning is similar for both kinds of blueberries. Leave them alone for two or three seasons, trimming only tangles or broken twigs. Then, to cut back a little on the extremely heavy crops of small berries, remove some of the oldest canes or stems and clip out a few of the fruiting twigs. If you do nothing, you will still get fruit, but it will be small and eventually decline in quantity.

Blueberries suffer from very few difficulties, but birds will take them all unless you net the plants. Nurseries carry suitable netting.

Always taste blueberries before picking. Some varieties look fully mature when still quite acid.

Approximately the same cultivars are used throughout the country, since the conditions for growing them are so similar.

Early cultivars. 'Earliblue'. Origin: New Jersey. One of the best for all areas, this berry is large, light blue, and firm. The picking scar is small, so fruit keeps well and resists cracking. Plants are upright and comparatively hardy. Good for all zones. Widely available.

'Ivanhoe'. One of the best berries, it is large, light blue, and firm. The plant is very tender. Good for the South. (2, 3, 26, 30)

'Northland'. Origin: Michigan. This is a very hardy variety. The fruit is medium-size, round, moderately firm, and medium blue. The flavor is good. The plant is spreading, reaching only 4 feet at maturity. Good for the North and West. Locally available.

'Weymouth'. Origin: New Jersey. The large, round berry has a dark blue skin and little aroma. It ripens very early and is best for cooking. The bush is erect, spreading, and very productive, but not vigorous. Good for the North and West. (2, 4)

Above left: Blueberries provide a good return in a small area—a few bushes will fill a pail.

Above: Netting over the plants allows blueberries to ripen before birds take them all—and reminds an eager child to wait patiently.

Midseason cultivars. 'Berkeley'. Origin: New Jersey. This very large, firm berry is pale blue and resists cracking. The bush is fairly upright and moderately hardy. Good for all zones, and especially for the West Coast into Northern California. Widely available.

'Bluecrop'. Origin: New Jersey. The fruit is large, light blue, and rather tart, but stores well and is good for cooking. The berries stand cold well, which makes the plant good for the shortest Michigan growing seasons. The plant is upright and medium hardy. Widely available.

'Bluecrop' blueberry

'Blueray'. Origin: New Jersey. The fruit is very large, firm, and sweet. The plant is upright and spreading. Good for all zones, and especially recommended for Washington. Widely available.

'Collins'. Origin: New Jersey. The fruit is large, light blue, firm, and sweet. It resists cracking. The plants are erect, well shaped, and fairly hardy, but not consistent in production. Good for the North and West. (27, 30)

'Croatan'. The fruit is medium-size and quick to ripen in warm weather. The plant is canker-resistant. Good for the South, and especially recommended for North Carolina. Locally available.

'Stanley'. Origin: New Jersey. This is a widely recommended variety. The fruit is medium-size and firm, with good color and flavor. The bush is hardy, vigorous, and upright. Since there are few main branches, pruning is easy. Good for the North and West. (2, 4, 7)

'Blueray' blueberry

Late cultivars. 'Coville'. Origin: New Jersey. This is an inconsistent variety with large light blue fruit that remains tart until near harvest. The plant is medium hardy. Good for all zones. Widely available.

'Delite'. This is the only variety that develops some sugar early, so picking is easier. The berries are medium large and may be reddish under the bloom. (6, 29, 41)

'Dixi'. Origin: New Jersey. The name is not an affectionate term for the South, but Latin for "I have spoken" or, loosely, "That's my last word." It was given by the developer, F. V. Coville, upon his retirement. The fruit is large, aromatic, flavorful, and good fresh.

'Menditoo'. This dark blue berry is large, medium firm, and sweet. The

'Dixi' blueberry

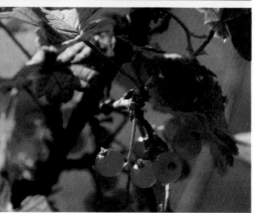

Both photographs, above: Red currants add great beauty to a garden, and they make delicious jelly.

bush is fairly vigorous and spreading. Fruit ripens over a long period, convenient for home gardeners. Locally available.

'Southland'. The firm, light blue berries have a waxy bloom, and may have tough skin late in the season. This is a good Gulf Coast plant. Locally available.

Currants and Gooseberries

As you can see from the photographs here, currants and gooseberries are among the most beautiful of the small fruits, but they are good home-garden shrubs for other reasons as well.

You won't often see fresh fruit in the market, since crops from the limited commercial plantings go to processors for commercial jellies and canned fruits. But since these plants are ornamental, easy to care for, and productive, northern gardeners can tuck a few among other shrubs—for the bloom, fruit, and fall color. The crop can be used for jelly and pie, or just fresh eating for those who like a tart fruit.

We discuss only the red and white currants of the species *Ribes sativum*, and the gooseberries, *Ribes uva-crispa* and *R. hirtellum*. The black currant, *Ribes nigrum*, so aromatic and rich in vitamin C, is unfortunately banned almost everywhere, since it is part of the disease cycle of white pine blister rust. The other *Ribes* species also take part in transferring this disease and they too are banned in some areas. Ask your nurseryman, and do not transport or plant any currant or gooseberry from outside your region without checking with your Cooperative Extension Office.

Fall or winter planting is a good idea, since the plants leaf out early. In cold climates, plant right after the leaves drop and the roots will establish before winter. Space the plants about 4 feet apart; or set them closer if more convenient, but expect them to grow less vigorously. If summer is hot, plant them against a north wall. In most areas, plant in the open, but be sure soil moisture is constant. Set the plants a little deeper than they grew in the nursery.

The plants are heavy feeders and require a regular program of feeding with nitrogen. The leaves will begin to yellow if soil nitrogen is low. Mulch will help keep weeds down and maintain constant moisture.

Almost any soil will do, but a rich, well-drained loam is best.

No pruning is necessary if you want only light crops on plants that are mainly ornamental. The plants bear the best fruit on the base of stems of the previous season, and on spurs along 2-year-old stems. To prune, remove stems that are more than 3 years old during the dormant season. You can leave 9 to 15 stems, depending upon the age of the plants.

Plants produce for up to 20 years in ideal climates, and less in warmer, southerly climates.

Currants are attacked by the usual aphids, mites, and so on, requiring occasional sprays (or hosing with water for mites). The most serious disease does not affect the currants themselves. Spores of white pine blister rust from miles away spend part of their lives on the currants, then transfer to pines growing within about 300 feet. Currants are banned where there is a white pine timber crop, but check your own and neighbors' gardens for pines with bundles of five needles, and if you find them, don't plant currants.

Currant cultivars. 'Perfection'. This old cultivar has medium-size red fruit in loose clusters. The plant has good foliage and is upright, vigorous, and productive. Good for Washington and Oregon. Widely available.

'Red Lake'. Origin: Minnesota. Recommended everywhere that currants will grow, this variety yields medium-to-large, light red berries in long, easy-to-pick clusters. The plants are slightly spreading. They produced the highest yield in Canadian trials and also produce well in California. Widely available.

'Stephens No. 9'. Origin: Ontario, Canada. This is a good Great Lakes cultivar with fairly large, medium-red berries in medium clusters. Plants are spreading and productive. Locally available.

'White Grape'. This is a white cultivar that is widely sold, but perhaps surpassed in quality by 'White Imperial', if you can find it. (31)

'Wilder'. This very old cultivar from Indiana yields dark red berries that are firm but tender, and very tart. Plants are large, hardy, and long-lived. (12, 13, 16, 24)

Gooseberry cultivars. 'Clark'. Origin: Ontario, Canada. The fruit is large and red when ripe. Plants are usually free of mildew. This is a good Canadian variety. (31)

'Fredonia'. Origin: New York. The large fruit is dark red when ripe. Plants are productive and vigorous, with open growth. (31)

'Oregon Champion'. Origin: Oregon. The medium-size fruit is green. This is a good variety for all West Coast growing areas. (3, 7, 14, 32)

'Pixwell'. Origin: North Dakota. This is a very hardy variety for Central and Plains States. The berries hang away from the plant, making them easy to pick, and the canes have few thorns. Widely available.

'Poorman'. An American type with red fruit, the plants are spiny and spreading. Good for the Pacific Northwest and the Central States. (27, 31)

Grapes

In the earliest periods of human history, four foods were recognizably important. In the North there were apples and honey. In the South there were olives and grapes.

The American grape entered our history more recently than the vine of Europe, but it has already played an important role, since its roots saved the European grape from extinction during the *Phylloxera* plague of the last century. More recently, American grapes have entered into sturdy hybrids that carry European wine grapes far north of their original climate area.

Above left: The pale American gooseberry reddens as it ripens.

Above right: 'White Imperial' or 'White Grape' cultivars produce large clusters of white currants.

Grapes send their roots deep where they can, and they prefer a soil that is rich in organic material. You can encourage growth by adding an organic supplement at planting time and mulching the roots afterward. The site should have good air circulation, because grapes are subject to disease where air is stagnant.

There are two kinds of grapes, and each is pruned differently. (See pages 68 and 69 for sketches and instructions.) In general, the *Americans* need cane pruning (long canes with 10 or more buds on each remain to fruit after pruning); and the *Europeans* need spur pruning (permanent arms or branches are developed, and canes along these are cut back to two buds). There are some exceptions, however.

Wine grapes (see page 130) are often trained to a head; that is, they are freestanding, with the fruiting stubs, or spurs, selected early—about 4 per vine—then clipped back each year until the leafless plant looks like a caveman's club.

Muscadines and bunch grapes (see pages 130–132) differ in pruning, once established.

Grapes need be fed only nitrogen, and may not always need that. If the leaves yellow and there is little growth in the early part of the season, they definitely need feeding. If you're not sure, try a feeding to see the result. Late feeding during the ripening period can force excessive growth and spoil the fruit.

Harvest grapes by taste and appearance. When you think the bunch looks ripe, taste a grape near the tip. If it's good, cut the bunch.

Sometimes grapes never taste sweet, no matter how long you wait. That simply means that you have planted the wrong variety for your area. Either switch to another variety, or replant the one you stubbornly insist on in a hot spot against a south wall or in a westward-facing corner.

Grapes mildew badly, and need good air circulation and treatment with a fungicide. The classic remedy is copper sulfate. A number of pests attack grapes, especially certain beetles. Birds love grapes, but you can save bunch grapes by placing the whole bunch in a paper bag.

Cultivars for the North. The American grapes are listed first, with a note when they are choice juice or wine grapes. French hybrids are listed second.

American grapes. 'Alden'. Origin: New York. The large clusters of reddish black berries are juicy, with fine aroma. The skin won't slip. The vine tends to overbear, so thin. Somewhat tender. (2, 3, 26, 27, 31)

'Bath'. Origin: New York. This cultivar bears medium clusters of black, juicy berries with no "foxy" flavor. The vine is fairly hardy and needs thinning. (2, 27, 31)

'Buffalo'. Origin: New York. This slipskin variety is good for wine or juice. The fairly large cluster holds reddish black fruit with a heavy surface bloom. The vine is vigorous and hardy. Widely available.

'Catawba'. Origin: North Carolina. Good for wine or juice, this red grape is a popular commercial variety. It requires a long season to ripen and will do well in southerly areas with the longest growing seasons. Thinning will hasten development. Widely available.

'Cayuga White'. This cultivar bears white grapes in tight clusters. They are of high dessert quality. (27)

'Concord'. Origin: Massachusetts. This late grape is so well known and widely planted that it hardly needs description. Often the standard of quality in judging American grapes, the dark blue slipskin berries are rich in the characteristic "foxy" flavor, which is retained after processing. Widely available.

'Delaware'. Origin: New Jersey. The clusters and berries of this major wine grape are small, good for wine and juice, and excellent for dessert eating. Vines mildew. (2, 8, 13, 22, 26, 28, 31, 33, 35)

'Fredonia'. Origin: New York. This cultivar should be allowed to set heav-

'Alden' grape

'Bath' grape

'Buffalo' grape

'Fredonia' grape

'New York Muscat' grape

'Schuyler' grape

ily, as it sometimes has difficulty with pollination. This is the top black grape in its season. Vines are hardy. Widely available.

'Himrod'. Origin: New York. This is the top white seedless grape throughout the northern states. 'Thompson' types replace it where weather is warmer. The vines are brittle and only moderately hardy. Widely available.

'New York Muscat'. Origin: New York. Good for wine and juice, the reddish-black berries in medium clusters have muscat aroma, which is rich and fruity. Temperatures below −15°F. can cause winter injury. (27, 31)

'Niagara'. Good for wine and juice, this is the most widely planted white grape and is even more productive than 'Concord'. It is vigorous and moderately hardy. Widely available.

'Schuyler'. Origin: New York. This grape resembles European grapes in flavor. It is soft and juicy with a tough skin. The vines are fairly hardy and disease resistant. (3, 26, 27)

'Seneca'. Origin: New York. The small-to-medium berries resemble European grapes, with tender golden skin and sweet, aromatic flavor. The vine is hardy and takes cane pruning, although one parent is a European type. (2, 26, 27, 31)

'Sheridan'. Origin: New York. Large berries have tough black skin and require a long season to mature. It is a 'Concord' type, and its vines are hardy. (2, 27, 31)

'Steuben'. Origin: New York. Blue-black berries grow in medium clusters' and are sweet and aromatic. The vine is productive, hardy, and disease resistant. Widely available.

'Van Buren'. Origin: New York. The small-to-medium clusters of jet-black grapes have a sweet, "foxy" flavor and are very good fresh. This is the earliest of 'Concord' types; however, the juice holds its flavor less well than 'Concord'. The vine is hardy but subject to mildew. (2, 3, 13, 19, 22, 27)

'Veesport'. Origin: Ontario, Canada. Borne in medium clusters, these black grapes are good for wine and juice, and acceptable for fresh eating. The vine is vigorous. (27)

'Seneca' grape

'Steuben' grape

'Van Buren' grape

French hybrids suitable for the North. Above from left to right: 'Aurora', 'Baco #1', 'Chancellor'. Below: 'DeChaunac'. Bottom: 'Foch'.

French hybrids. Spur-prune these. They are hybrids of European and less well known American grapes (not the 'Concord' type, *Vitis labrusca*). All are for wine or juice, but good fresh.

'Aurora' (Seibel 5279). This very early white grape is soft, with a pleasant flavor. It is moderately productive and grows far better in sandy rather than heavy soils. Choose it if early ripening is needed. Widely available.

'Baco #1' ('Baco Noir'). This midseason cultivar produces small clusters of small black grapes. It is extremely vigorous and productive. Widely available.

'Chancellor' (Seibel 7053). This vigorous blue-fruited grape ripens in late midseason. The vines produce well even though they are subject to downy mildew. (2, 27)

'De Chaunac' (Seibel 9549). This midseason variety is one of the best blues, especially for home winemaking. The clusters are medium to large on vigorous and productive vines. (2, 6, 13, 26, 27)

'Foch'. This very early black variety bears medium-size clusters, with medium berries. Birds love them, so protect the crop. Vines are very vigorous. (2, 3, 6, 26, 27)

Seyve Villard 12-375. For table use as well as wine, these white berries ripen in late midseason. The vines are vigorous, productive, and hardy. (2, 27)

Seyve Villard 5276. An early cultivar with large and compact bunches of white berries, it is subject to downy mildew and black rot. (2, 22, 27)

Cultivars for the West. The West is grape country, wherever you go, yet many gardeners are disappointed in the fruit they harvest from their vines. The problem is usually a poor choice of varieties. Grapes, more than any other fruit, require the right climate and amount of heat to produce well. Too many gardeners buy vines because they like the fruit in the market, or because they know a famous name.

In general, western grape climates are divided into three groups. The first includes all of the West except California and the Southwestern desert. Gardeners in these cool regions should choose an American grape of the "foxy"-flavored species, *Vitis labrusca*. The most highly recommended appear below under the heading, "Northwest". One famous name often sold by nurserymen in the cool regions is not successful in western Washington and Oregon—that is 'Concord'. It requires more heat.

In California, the cooler coastal areas and coastal valleys are suited to American grapes and selected European varieties with a low-heat requirement. 'Concord' does well, but the popular 'Thompson Seedless' will almost always disappoint a gardener. The variety named 'Perlette' is similar, but was developed for the low heat of this climate. The inland Northwest, and parts of Utah, Colorado, and Idaho, can also use 'Concord' and 'Niagara' from the California coast list.

In the hot inner valleys of the Coast Range, there are major commercial vineyards growing all the renowned European wine varieties. The Napa–Sonoma wine region is well known, but there are wine grapes in newer plantings in southern Santa Clara County, San Benito County, near Salinas, and north of Santa Barbara.

The very hot Central Valley climate is perfect for the European table grapes you find in markets. 'Thompson', 'Ribier', and 'Emperor' all do well.

The low and high deserts are not good grape country. The earliest-maturing European varieties stand the best chance of producing a worthwhile crop.

Listed here are cultivars by region.

Northwest. 'Buffalo'. See "Cultivars for the North."

'Interlaken Seedless'. Origin: New York. This variety ripens early, with medium clusters of small, seedless berries with greenish-white skin that adheres. The flesh is crisp and sweet. The grape resembles 'Thompson Seedless', but has interesting flavor overtones. The vine is fairly hardy and best with cane pruning. Widely available.

'Ontario'. Origin: Canada. These white berries form in fairly loose clusters. The vines are vigorous, productive, fairly hardy, and prefer quite heavy soils. Cane pruning is best. (6, 26, 27, 31)

'Schuyler'. See "Cultivars for the North."

'Seneca'. See "Cultivars for the North."

'Van Buren'. See "Cultivars for the North."

California coast. 'Cardinal'. Origin: California. These large, dark red grapes ripen early and have firm, greenish flesh. The medium-size clusters are extremely abundant, to three per cane, but irregular. The vine can run rampant. Use it to cover an arbor or summerhouse. Spur pruning is best. (14, 42)

'Concord'. This grape, described earlier, does not like high California heat or the coolest Northwest summers, but does well anywhere in between. Cane pruning is best. Widely available.

'Delight'. Origin: California. This grape ripens early, yielding well-filled clusters of large, greenish yellow berries with firm flesh and a distinct muscatlike flavor. Spur pruning is best. Locally available.

'Niabell'. Origin: California. This midseason cultivar produces well-filled clusters of large, black berries good fresh or as juice. Vines are vigorous, resist powdery mildew, and can be pruned to long canes. Cane pruning is best. (10, 45)

'Niagara'. This variety, described earlier, ripens midseason to late midseason. Cane pruning is best. Widely available.

'Perlette'. Origin: California. This early cultivar bears large, compact clusters of white to yellowish grapes that are very tender and juicy with mild flavor. They tolerate high temperatures, but also ripen where overall heat is fairly low. The vine is vigorous, very fruitful, and needs thinning. Spur pruning is best. Locally available.

'Pierce'. If 'Van Buren' is the cool-summer 'Concord', then this is the hot-summer 'Concord'. Grow it in the warmer regions of Central California where you want a "foxy" black slipskin. The vine is very vigorous. Cane pruning is best. Locally available.

Hot climates, California valleys. 'Cardinal'. See above.

'Emperor'. This late-ripening, large, red grape has flesh so firm it seems to crunch. It is adapted to the hottest part of the valley. In cooler valley regions you can obtain a similar fruit by planting 'Tokay'. Cane or spur pruning is best. (14)

'Interlaken Seedless' grape

'Perlette' grape

'Tokay' grape

'Cabernet Sauvignon' grape

'Muscat of Alexandria'. These late-midseason, large, green berries dappled with amber and in loose clusters are not pretty, but have an unparalleled musky, rich flavor. They lose flavor if held too long, so are best eaten fresh from the home garden. Spur pruning is best. (Muscats are often used to make sweet dessert wine. The nonfortified muscat wine is a real treat with desserts or fruit.) (14, 42)

'Niabell'. See above. This is a juice grape. Locally available.

'Perlette'. See above. Try this one in low desert regions as it is resistant to sunscald. Locally available.

'Red Malaga'. This early midseason variety bears large clusters filled with large pink-to-reddish purple berries that have little flavor. Use spur pruning or cane pruning with thinning of flowers. Locally available.

'Ribier'. This is a beautiful, early midseason dessert grape with very large, jet-black berries. They tend to soften quickly in storage and lose their mild flavor. The vines are overproductive. Use spur pruning and thin the flowers. (14, 42)

'Scarlet'. The compact clusters of this midseason variety hold jet-black berries with abundant, bright red juice that is sweet and richly flavored. It also has a mild "foxy" flavor. Vines are vigorous and ideal for arbors. Leaves turn dark red in fall. Cane pruning is best. Locally available.

'Thompson Seedless'. This is the top commercial seedless green grape, ripening in early midseason. Clusters are well filled with rather long fruit; and the flavor is mild. Grow only in hot climates. (Try 'Perlette' or 'Delight' if in doubt.) Cane pruning is best. (14, 42)

'Tokay'. This late midseason variety bears large clusters of large, very firm red grapes that are attractive but have little flavor. It does well in the Lodi area and the cooler valley climates. Use 'Emperor' in hotter climates. Spur pruning is best. Locally available.

Wine grapes. The list includes three of the best-known cultivars. They change character over short distances, so unless you know that professionals grow them near you, don't count on getting the best quality wines. Other well-known but hard-to-find California wine grapes are pictured on this page.

'Cabernet Sauvignon'. This is the great European black grape used to make the Bordeaux wines of France. (14)

'Pinot Noir'. This small black grape is used to make the French Burgundy wines. Difficult to handle. (14, 34, 40)

'Zinfandel'. This is a California specialty for red wine. You can probably grow this better than any other, as it seems to make drinkable wine in a variety of climates. (14, 40)

Cultivars for the South. In the South, two quite different types of grapes are widely grown, both of American origin. The bunch grape is typified by 'Concord'. Although this type prefers a cool climate, cultivars are available

Right: 'Pinot Noir' grape
Far right: 'Zinfandel' grape

for most regions. The real southern grape is, of course, the muscadine, with its smaller clusters of berries and a liking for Cotton Belt weather.

The bunch grapes are listed first, with a mention of the best zone if they are limited. The muscadines are best suited to warmer areas.

Bunch grapes. 'Catawba'. This grape described earlier, is especially recommended for South Carolina. Widely available.

'Champanel'. These large, purple grapes grow in clusters that are long but sometimes poorly filled. The berries are large and juicy, with high acidity. Vines are vigorous and productive. Locally available.

'Concord'. See "Cultivars for the North."

'Delaware'. See "Cultivars for the North."

'Fredonia'. See "Cultivars for the North."

'Golden Muscat' grape

'Golden Muscat'. Origin: New York. These large, golden berries are borne in large clusters. The flavor is typically rich and fruity—muscat, not "foxy". Vines are tender. It is especially recommended for Georgia. (2)

'Himrod'. See "Cultivars for the North."

'Niagara'. See "Cultivars for the North."

'Seneca'. See "Cultivars for the North."

'Steuben'. See "Cultivars for the North."

Muscadines. Many muscadines are sterile and need a pollinator. The cultivars below described as "perfect" will pollinate themselves and any other variety.

'Bountiful'. Origin: North Carolina. Perfect. These reddish black berries are borne in clusters of one to six. The flavor is sweet and sprightly. Vines are disease resistant. (20, 29, 35, 39)

'Carlos'. Origin: North Carolina. Perfect. Bronze berries in medium-size clusters have a 'Scuppernong' flavor, good fresh or as juice. The vines are hardy and resist many diseases. (2, 20, 29, 35, 39)

Well-suited to warm areas, muscadines are special favorites in the South.

'Cowart'. Origin: Georgia. Perfect. Black berries, ripening very late in large clusters, have good flavor. The vine is productive and somewhat tolerant of insects and disease. (20, 29, 39)

'Dearing'. Origin: North Carolina. Perfect. This fairly late variety has green skin and rather crisp flesh. The flavor is sweet, the best of the perfect varieties. (2, 29, 39)

'Higgins'. Origin: Georgia. The large, compact cluster ripens in midseason. The bronze berries are soft and good. Vines are outstandingly productive and moderately resistant to black rot. (20, 29, 35, 39, 41)

'Hunt'. Origin: Georgia. This dull black fruit is unusual in ripening evenly. The quality is excellent, high in sugar, and very good for wine and juice. This cultivar is unanimously recommended for home and commercial planting by the Muscadine Grape Committee. (2, 20, 29, 39, 41)

'Jumbo'. This is a very large black muscadine of good quality. It ripens over several weeks, so is excellent for home use fresh. Vines are disease resistant. (20, 29, 35, 39)

'Magoon'. Origin: Mississippi. Perfect. Reddish purple berries are medium-size and have a sprightly and aromatic flavor. The vine is productive and vigorous. (29, 31, 41)

'Scuppernong'. Origin: North Carolina. This is the true muscadine, the earliest variety named. Most people call any similar grape a scuppernong, but this is the real cultivar. Fruit color varies from greenish to reddish bronze, depending on sun. It is late-ripening, sweet, and juicy, with aromatic flavor. Good for eating fresh or for wine or juice. (2, 20, 29, 33, 35)

'Southland'. Origin: Mississippi. Perfect. This very large grape is purple and dull-skinned, with good flavor and high sugar content. The vine is moderately vigorous and productive. Good for the central and southern portions of the Gulf Coast states. (20, 29, 39, 41)

'Thomas'. This standard grape has reddish black, small-to-medium berries that are very sweet and excellent for fresh juice. Locally available.

'Topsail'. Origin: North Carolina. Clusters of three to five berries have green fruit splotched with bronze. This is the sweetest of all muscadines and very good for fresh use. It is often a poor producer. Vines are not very hardy, but are disease resistant. (29, 39)

'Yuga'. Origin: Georgia. These reddish bronze berries are sweet and of excellent quality, but ripen late and irregularly. They are fine for home gardens. (29, 39)

Strawberries

If you have grown strawberries for any length of time, you know that flavor and yield are not exactly predictable, but vary from year to year depending upon spring growing conditions. Also, if you have gardened in several locations you know that the best variety in one place may be only fair in another. A good nurseryman can be a big help, since he'll keep abreast of developments in plant breeding and offer plants that should succeed. Your county agricultural agent can help too, especially if you've had trouble in other seasons.

Strawberries can be grown in either the matted-row or the hill system. There are two types of matted rows. In one, all runners are allowed to grow; in the other, only the earliest to form remain, spaced about 8 inches apart. The latter, spaced-runner system gives you larger berries, easier picking, and larger total yield. See the illustration for the arrangement of runners. The rows should be spaced 3 to 4 feet apart when you plant.

In the hill system, plants are 12 inches apart in the row and all runners are picked off. The rows are spaced about 12 to 15 inches apart in groups of three. Each group is separated by an aisle 24 to 30 inches wide so that you can walk among the plants to pick or care for them. This system lends itself to everbearing strawberries, or single-crop kinds that don't send out many runners.

Planting Strawberries

Plant strawberries in a double-row hill system with furrows on the outside or in a single row with space on either side of the plants for the runners to establish into the matted row system.

Plant strawberies with the roots spread in a fan shape. Keep the crown above the soil line.

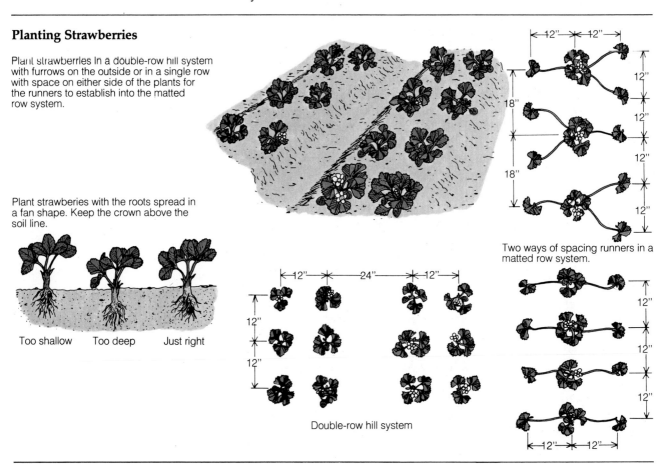

Too shallow   Too deep   Just right

Two ways of spacing runners in a matted row system.

Double-row hill system

To encourage vigorous growth of regular cultivars, remove blossoms that appear the year the plants are set out. The year that everbearing kinds are planted, remove all blossoms until the middle of July. The later blossoms will produce a late-summer and fall crop.

Plant strawberries in soil with good drainage, and mound the planting site if you're not sure. See the illustration on page 132 for proper planting depth. The new leaf bud in the center of each plant should sit exactly level with the soil surface.

Gardeners who grow strawberries in containers in a disease-free soil mix don't have to worry about verticillium wilt and red stele (root rot). Both are caused by soilborne fungus. When growing strawberries in containers or in garden soil, ask for plants that are certified as disease free.

Winter protection is needed where alternate freezing and thawing of the soil may cause the plants to heave and break the roots. Low temperatures also injure the crowns of the plants.

Place a straw mulch 3 or 4 inches deep over the plants before the soil is frozen hard. Remove most of the mulch in spring when the center of a few plants shows a yellow-green color. You can leave an inch of loose straw, even add some fresh straw between rows. The plants will come up through it and it will help retain moisture in the soil and keep mud off the berries.

In northern areas, and as far south as North Carolina, strawberries should be set out in early spring. In the warmer regions of North Carolina, plants can be set out in fall or winter as well, and you can expect a light crop from these plants about 5 months later.

In northern Cotton Belt climates, set plants in September for the highest yield of spring berries. Waiting until later will diminish the crop.

In the warmest Gulf climates and into zone 2 and Florida, you must order cold-stored plants, or plants from the north, for planting from February to March. You can also obtain a quick crop by planting northern plants in early November for winter fruiting, but the crop will be smaller. The runners from February plantings can be transplanted in May and August to increase the size of your planting.

Western planting seasons impose unique restrictions on strawberry growth.

In the coldest areas of zone 7 (California) and zones 6 and 7 (Great Basin to Colorado), plant as early in spring as possible, since there is good moisture in the soil to start the plants. If soils are usually too mucky, protect a mounded bed with plastic to keep it friable.

In the Northwest, especially the coolest areas of western Washington, plant early in fall so plants can become established before real cold sets in, or else wait until early spring. Watch for washouts from heavy fall rain. Weed carefully in spring so weeds don't compete.

In California, plant in fall in cold-winter zones 12, 13, and 9, but get the plants in early in zone 9. In mild-winter zones 10 and 11, use chilled plants (stored at 34°F. for a short period) and set them out in October and November. The low desert is a chancy area for strawberries, but October planting may give results.

Anywhere in California, the berries will do better with a plastic mulch, which increases winter soil temperature and holds water well.

Cultivars for the North and South. 'Albritton'. Origin: North Carolina. This late berry is large and uniform in size, and excellent fresh and for freezing. It develops a rich flavor in North Carolina. (14, 30, 43)

'Ardmore'. Origin: Missouri. These large, late midseason berries are yellowish red outside, lighter inside, and have good flavor. Plants are productive in heavy silt loam. A northern cultivar. (4, 13, 30)

'Blakemore'. Origin: Maryland introduction. These early berries are small and firm, with a high acid and pectin content. They have fair flavor but are excellent for preserves. Plants are vigorous, with good runner production

Container-grown strawberries planted in a disease-free soil mix stay healthy. The bigger the container, the larger the yield.

Top: Wire-screen row covers protect strawberry fruits from birds.

Above: Screen the plants before the berries ripen.

and high resistance to virus diseases and verticillium wilt. They are adapted to a wide range of soil types from Virginia to Georgia, and westward to Oklahoma and southern Missouri. (4, 6, 43)

'Catskill'. These large midseason berries are of good dessert quality and excellent for freezing. The fruit is not firm enough for distance shipping, but the plant is a productive home-garden variety. It is grown over a wide range of soil types from New England and New Jersey to southern Minnesota. Also good for the South. (2, 4, 6, 13, 26, 30, 35, 43)

'Cyclone'. Origin: Iowa. This variety yields large berries with very good flavor that are also good for freezing. The plant is hardy, resists foliage diseases, and is well adapted to North Central States. Widely available.

'Daybreak'. Origin: Louisiana. These medium-red berries are large and very attractive, with good flavor and preserving quality. Plants are very productive. Good throughout the South. Locally available.

'Dixieland'. This early berry is deep red, firm, acid in flavor, and excellent for freezing. Plants are sturdy and vigorous. Good for the South.

'Dunlap'. Origin: Illinois. This early-to-midseason berry is medium-size with dark crimson skin and deep red flesh. It does not ship well but is a good home-garden fruit. Plants are hardy and adapted to a wide range of soil types in northern Illinois, Iowa, Wisconsin, Minnesota, North Dakota, South Dakota, and Nebraska. (11, 12, 13, 16, 19)

'Earlibelle'. This widely adapted early variety produces large, very firm fruit that is good for canning and freezing. Plants are medium-size, with good runner production and resistance to leaf spot and leaf scorch. Good for all zones. (2, 4, 30, 43)

'Earlidawn'. This is an early market and freezing strawberry. Berries are large and of good dessert quality. Moderately resistant to leaf spot and leaf scorch. It is adapted to Maryland, north to New England. (2, 4, 6, 13, 43)

'Fairfax'. Origin: Maryland. This attractive, medium-size, early mid-season berry is bright red outside, deep red inside. The flavor is excellent. Plants are especially productive when late-season runners are picked off. They are grown from southern New England to Maryland. (2, 4, 6, 13, 26, 30)

'Fletcher'. Origin: New York. Berries are medium in size, with a medium-red, glossy, tender skin. Flavor is excellent. Very good for freezing. Plants are well adapted to New York and New England. (13, 30)

'Florida 90'. Origin: Florida. Berries are very large, with very good flavor and quality. The plant is a heavy producer of fruit and runners. (30, 41, 43)

'Guardian'. These large, deep red, midseason berries are firm, uniform in size, and attractive. They have good dessert quality and freeze well. Plants are vigorous, productive, and resist many diseases. Good throughout the South. (2, 4, 6, 8, 12, 13, 19, 30, 43)

'Headliner'. Origin: Louisiana. These midseason berries are of good quality. Plants are vigorous and productive, make runners freely, and resist leaf spot. A southern cultivar. Locally available.

'Howard 17' ('Premier'). Origin: Massachusetts. These are early, medium-size berries of good quality. Plants are productive and resistant to leaf diseases and virus disease. Locally available in the Northeast.

'Jerseybelle'. Origin: New Jersey. Noted for its large, showy fruits, this variety has a mild flavor but is not adapted to freezing. Plants are highly susceptible to diseases. (2, 4, 6, 8, 13)

'Marlate'. This very large, attractive fruit is good fresh and freezes well. The plant is extremely hardy, and is, therefore, a productive and dependable late variety. Does well in the South. (2, 4, 6, 13, 30, 43)

'Midland'. Origin: Maryland. This very early variety bears large, glossy berries with deep red flesh. They are good to excellent for fresh use, and freeze well. The plant does best when grown in the hill system. It is adapted from southern New England to Virginia, and west to Iowa and Kansas. (2, 13)

'Midway'. Origin: Maryland. These large berries are of good to very good dessert quality and good for freezing. Plants are susceptible to leaf spot, leaf scorch, and verticillium wilt. They are widely planted in Michigan. Widely available.

'Missionary'. The medium-soft-to-firm fruit of this midseason cultivar is dark crimson, acid in flavor, and of fair quality. It is good for preserves or freezing. The plant does well anywhere in Georgia. Locally available.

'Pocahontas'. Origin: Maryland. This variety is good fresh, frozen, or in preserves. Plants are vigorous and resist leaf scorch. They are adapted to southern New England and south to Norfolk. (2, 4, 6, 13, 30, 33, 34, 41, 43)

'Raritan'. Origin: New Jersey. These midseason berries are large, firm, and have good flavor. Plants are medium size. (2, 4, 6, 19)

'Redchief'. The fruit is medium to large and of uniform deep-red color, with a firm, glossy surface. The plant is extremely productive and very resistant to red stele. Good for the South. (2, 4, 6, 8, 13, 30, 43)

'Redstar'. Origin: Maryland. These late berries are large and of good to very good dessert quality. Plants resist virus disease, leaf spot, and leaf scorch. They are grown from southern New England, south to Maryland, and west to Missouri and Iowa. (2, 4, 13)

'Sparkle'. This is a productive midseason variety, with bright red, attractive berries that are fairly soft and have good flavor. Berry size is good in early picking, but small in later ones. Widely available in the North.

'Sunrise'. Origin: Maryland. Berries are medium in size, symmetrical, and firm, with very good flavor. The flesh is too pale for freezing. A vigorous grower, the plant resists red stele, leaf scorch, and mildew. (2, 4, 5, 8, 12, 30, 33, 41, 43)

'Surecrop'. Origin: Maryland. This early berry is large, round, glossy, firm, and of good dessert quality. Large plants should be spaced 6 to 9 inches apart for top production. It is resistant to red stele, verticillium wilt, leaf spot, leaf scorch, and drought. Good in all zones. Widely available.

Top: 'Midway' strawberry
Above: 'Sparkle' strawberry

'Suwanee'. This is a medium to large, early, tender berry of very good quality, both fresh or frozen. It is a very poor shipper, but excellent for the home garden. Locally available in the South.

'Tennessee Beauty'. This late berry is medium-size, attractive, glossy red, firm, and has good flavor. It is good for freezing. Plants are productive in fruit and runners. They resist leaf spot, leaf scorch, and virus diseases. (2, 13, 30, 35, 41, 43)

'Trumpeter'. Origin: Minnesota. These medium-size late berries are soft and glossy and have very good flavor. This is a winter-hardy and productive home-garden variety for the upper Mississippi Valley and Plains States. (16)

Everbearing cultivars for the North and South. 'Gem' ('Superfection' and 'Brilliant' are considered to be nearly identical to 'Gem'). This variety yields small, glossy red, tart fruit of good dessert quality. Widely available.

'Geneva'. Large, vigorous plants fruit well in June and throughout the summer and early autumn. Berries are soft and highly flavored. (4, 6, 12, 13)

'Ogallala'. Berries are dark red, soft, and of medium size, have good flavor, and are good for freezing. Plants are vigorous and hardy. Widely available.

'Ozark Beauty'. An everbearing variety for the cooler climate zones, this one produces poorly in mild climates. The berries are bright red inside and out, are large, sweet, and have good flavor. In any one season, only the mother plants produce, yielding crops in the summer and fall. Runner plants produce the following season. Widely available.

Cultivars for the West

The Rockies and the Great Basin. Recommended for these areas are these varieties, described earlier: 'Cyclone', 'Dunlap', 'Gem', 'Ogallala', 'Ozark Beauty', 'Sparkle', and 'Trumpeter'.

Western Washington and Oregon. 'Hood'. Origin: Oregon. These mid-

In the Pacific Northwest, 'Olympus' produces very large fruit on vigorous plants.

A plastic mulch helps retain water and warm the soil.

'Sequoia' strawberry

season berries are large, conical, bright red, and glossy. They are held high in strong, upright clusters, and are good fresh or in preserves. Plants are resistant to mildew but somewhat susceptible to red stele. (3, 36, 40)

'Northwest'. Origin: Washington. Late midseason fruit is large at first, then smaller, with crimson skin and red flesh. It is firm, well flavored, and good fresh, in preserves, or for freezing. Plants are very productive and so resistant to virus diseases that they can be planted where virus has killed other varieties. (3, 36)

'Olympus'. Origin: Washington. Late midseason fruit is held well-up on arching stems. Berries are medium to large, bright red throughout, tender, and firm. Plants are vigorous but produce few runners. They resist red stele and virus diseases, but are somewhat susceptible to botrytis infection. (36, 40)

'Puget Beauty'. Origin: Washington. The large, glossy, very attractive fruit has light crimson skin. Flesh is highly flavored, excellent fresh, and good for freezing and preserves. Plants are large and upright, with moderate runner production. They resist mildew but are somewhat susceptible to red stele. Locally available.

'Quinault'. An everbearer with a moderate early crop, heavier in July–September. The fruit is very large and soft, with good color. The plant produces good runners. (2, 3, 14, 40)

'Rainier'. These late midseason berries are large, firm, and of good quality. Plants are very vigorous, with large leaf blades but moderate runner production. (3, 36, 40)

'Shuksan'. This midseason cultivar bears very large, firm berries that are bright red, glossy, and broadly wedge-shaped. Fruit is good for freezing, and plants are vigorous. (3, 36, 40)

California. 'Fresno'. Origin: California. Large, uniform, midseason fruit is light red and very good fresh. The plant is very vigorous, producing many runners, and tolerates salinity. It is good for Southern California. (10, 14)

'Salinas'. Origin: California. The skin of this midseason berry is red with a bright finish. The flesh is light to bright red and firm, with excellent flavor. The medium-size plant is productive with profuse runners, and resists verticillium wilt. It is recommended for the central coast Locally available.

'Sequoia'. Origin: California. This is an early variety that may even bear in December. The exceptionally large fruit is dark red, tender with soft flesh, and has excellent flavor. Harvest frequently for best quality. The plant is erect and vigorous, with many runners. It is recommended for winter planting along the central and south coast. Widely available.

'Shasta'. Origin: California. This large midseason berry is bright red and glossy with firm red flesh, good for freezing or preserves. Plants are fairly vigorous, with moderate numbers of runners. They have some resistance to mildew and virus diseases. Locally available.

'Tioga'. Origin: California. This early berry is medium-red and glossy, with firm flesh that is fine for preserves or freezing. The plant is vigorous, moderately resistant to virus, and fairly tolerant of salinity, but highly susceptible to verticillium wilt. It is good for late-summer planting. (2, 6, 13)

'Torrey'. Origin: California. Large, uniform, early fruit has dark red skin and firm flesh. The vigorous plant produces numerous runners, resists virus, and tolerates salinity. It is especially good for Southern California. Locally available.

Subtropical Fruits

The following plants are all considered subtropical. None of them will tolerate much frost. However, jujube, kiwi, and loquat will tolerate cold well enough to be planted anywhere along the Gulf Coast, and the feijoa will grow as far north as Atlanta. Loquat and kiwi are sometimes successful in protected areas on the East Coast as far north as Washington D.C. In the West, avocado, carissa, feijoa, jujube, and loquat will grow as far north as San Francisco Bay. Kiwi will grow as far north as Portland, Oregon. All others are tender and will not do well outside zone 1 in the South, or north of Santa Barbara in the West.

Hardy subtropicals. Avocado (*Persea americana*). Two avocado cultivars, 'Bacon' and 'Zutano', will fruit in cool regions, especially if they have a good exposure and protection from wind. 'Bacon' is preferred. In milder regions from Monterey Bay to San Diego you can plant the black-fruited 'Haas', the green 'Fuerte', and other tender cultivars.

Jujube (*Ziziphus jujuba*). An attractive and fairly hardy tree, the jujube produces a round or pear-shaped fruit that is good fresh or will dry on the tree. Dried, it resembles a date; hence the common name, "Chinese date." There are two cultivars: 'Lang' is pear-shaped; 'Li' is round. The tree thrives in alkaline soil.

Kiwi (*Actinidia chinensis*). This furry, egg-sized fruit is being found increasingly in supermarkets. It has emerald-green flesh with an unusual, but delicious, flavor. The fruit grows on a sturdy vine that can live even in snowy climates. It is most tender when the young growth sprouts in spring, when it must have night protection. You must have both male and female kiwi vines for fruit. Prune and train them like spur grapes. Try 'Hayward', 'Monty', or 'Bruno'.

Loquat (*Eriobotrya japonica*). This is usually an ornamental tree, but with enough heat, named varieties produce delicious fruit. The leaves are large, wooly, and striking, and the tree is hardy and drought-tolerant. Try 'Champagne' and 'Gold Nugget'. Fireblight can kill it quick.

Natal plum (*Carissa grandiflora*). These beautiful but thorny plants range from tall shrubs to groundcover dwarfs. They produce single white, very fragrant flowers and plum-colored, cranberry-flavored fruit. They are widely available as ornamentals.

Pineapple guava (*Feijoa sellowiana*). Tall shrubs or small trees, these relatively hardy plants have silver-backed leaves and striking flowers with sweet and edible petals. The fruit needs heat to be good. It is small, oval, and yellow, and good fresh or in jam. A good cultivar is 'Coolidge'.

Tender subtropicals. Barbados cherry (*Malpighia glabra*). This is a large, densely branched shrub that can be clipped to make a hedge or 10- to 12-foot screen. It bears pale pink to rose flowers in April, followed by fruits in May. Flowering and fruiting continues through summer and fall. Look for named varieties. Fruit from seedlings varies from sweet to tart. Fruit is used in preserves, jellies, ices, beverages, and in making wine.

Cherimoya (*Annona cherimola*). This fruit has large, bumpy scales. Inside, the pulp is a spicy white custard, hence another common name, custard apple. You have to pollinate by hand if you want a good crop. Cold-climate gardeners can try the related fruit called pawpaw (*Asimina triloba*), from eastern North America. If you can find a named variety, buy it. Most are seedlings. The tree grows to 15 feet.

Jaboticaba (*Myrciaria cauliflora*). Attractive in form and foliage, and amenable to pruning and clipping as a hedge, this large shrub, or small tree, would deserve a place in the home landscape even without its spectacular fruiting habit. The grapelike fruits are borne singly or in twos or threes on the trunk and larger branches. The fruit has a thin tough skin. The flesh is white, juicy, and gelatinous with a few small seeds. It has a pleasant, sprightly grape flavor when ripe, freezes well, and is also used for making a superior jelly, for juice, and for winemaking.

Jack fruit (*Artocarpus heterophyllus*). This giant-size fruit grows on a modest-size tree with handsome, dark green, glossy foliage. Fruit ranges from 12 to 20 inches long and 6 to 8 inches thick, weighing 20 to 30 pounds. The whitish pulp of the fruit is edible but not exciting. The fruit pays its way

Top: Crushed passion fruit (*Passiflora edulis*) gives a delicious juice for drinks or sherbets.

Above: Pineapple guava (*Feijoa sellowiana*) is delicious fresh or in jams or fruit salads.

Frost-tender strawberry guava (*Psidium littorale* var. *longipes*) makes fine jellies.

Very tender soursop (*Annona muricata*) requires a near-tropical growing climate.

with its numerous nutlike seeds, which, when roasted, are a much-enjoyed delicacy throughout the tropics.

Lychee (*Litchi chinensis*). This tree is well worth planting for its appearance, even if you don't want the fruit. It is a large evergreen that covers itself with red fruit clusters each year. With the red husk removed, the white fruit is perfumed and delcious fresh, or it can be dried or canned.

Mango (*Mangifera indica*). This is one of the finest tropical fruits. Flavor varies widely, so plant a named variety for a handsome shade tree that is somewhat like a peach tree, and bears fruit that defies description. Some of the slightly green crop can be reserved for pie or preserves.

Papaya (*Carica papaya*). This is a small succulent-stemmed tree to about 20 feet. Most types do not branch, but develop huge leaves with hollow stems at the top of the hollow trunk. A well-grown tree will begin to bear fruit a year after planting. Older cultivars require both male and female trees, but newer varieties have bisexual flowers. Improved cultivar selections 'Solo', 'Sunrise', and 'X-77' are generally available. 'X-77' has the most attractive form.

Passion fruit (*Passiflora edulis*). There are several passion vines, but this is the one for fruit, either purple or yellow. Grow the vine on an arbor, admire the purple and white bloom, then crush juice from the fruit for drinks and sherbet.

Sapodilla (*Manilkara zapota*). This handsome, symmetrical tree has a strong central leader and whorled leaves at the ends of its branches, creating a dense, spreading canopy. Round fruits and those shaped like eggs vary from 2 to 4 inches in diameter. Flesh is smooth to granular in texture, with a sweet flavor. Fruit is used fresh—never cooked. It may be pulped for use in sherbets and ice cream. To get quality fruit, avoid seedling trees. Choose one of the named varieties.

Seagrape (*Coccoloba unifera*). This is a picturesque large shrub or small tree that grows to 20 to 30 feet tall. Fruits are used in making jelly and a potent wine. Seagrape jelly has an interesting musky flavor, and a distinctive light lavender color. Some fruits are quite acid, others insipid or sweet. The only way to be sure of fruit quality is to propagate from a plant of superior quality.

Soursop (*Annona muricata*). An oddity that produces 3- to 6-pound fruit on a small, upright tree. It's very tender, for warmest zone 1. You open the fruit to find white, pulpy flesh. Squeeze out the juice for a refreshing drink ingredient. It is sour, as its name implies.

Strawberry guava (*Psidium littorale* var. *longipes*). The strawberry guava is a handsome shrub or small tree, and produces a crop of small red or yellow fruit that is good fresh and excellent for jellies. It is a better-looking garden plant than the common, or lemon guava (var. *littorale*), which grows larger, but with a less attractive form. The yellow fruit may have white, pink, or yellow flesh, which has a very special flavor popular for jelly.

Surinam cherry (*Eugenia uniflora*). This evergreen shrub has enjoyed popularity as a handsome and useful landscape plant. With the introduction of varieties with improved fruit qualities, its value as a fruiting plant has been recognized. The fruits are used in making jams and jellies, syrup, compote, wine, and sherbets.

List of Catalog Sources

The numbers in the varieties lists correspond to the numbered sources below. The descriptions tell you which companies are specialists in fruits and which cover a large spectrum of garden materials. Many of these firms issue catalogs which are the equivalents of garden books, serving as excellent reference sources for the careful reader.

If not marked otherwise, sources are retail. Wholesale nurseries will not sell directly to you, but you can refer your nurseryman to them as sources for plants you want.

Adams County Nursery & Fruit Farms (1)
Aspers, PA 17304
Fruit specialists. Wholesale and retail.

Bountiful Ridge Nurseries, Inc. (2)
Princess Anne, MD 21853
Specialists in fruits and nuts. Catalog includes planting guide. Wholesale and retail.

Bowers Berry Nursery (3)
94959 Hwy 99 E
Junction City, OR 97448
Catalog of berries and grapes. Wholesale and retail.

Bunting's Berries (4)
Selbyville, DE 19975
Fruit trees, berries, and nursery stock.

Burgess Seed and Plant Co. (5)
P.O. Box 82
Galesburg, MI 49053
Two catalogs are offered: a general seed catalog, with flowers, vegetables, fruit, and nursery stock; and a full color catalog especially for the limited-space gardener, with a page on fruits to grow indoors.

W. Atlee Burpee Co. (6)
Warminster, PA 18974
General seed catalog. Flowers, vegetables, fruit, garden aids, and nursery stock.

C & O Nursery (7)
P.O. Box 116
1700 N. Wenatchee Ave.
Wenatchee, WA 98801
Fruit specialists, exclusive patented varieties. Catalog includes ornamentals and shade trees. Wholesale and retail.

The Clyde Nursery (8)
Highway U.S. 20
Clyde, OH 43410
Catalog of fruits and berries.

Columbia Basin Nursery (9)
Box 458
Quincy, WA 98848
Colored brochure and price list. Seedling rootstock, dwarfing apple rootstock, dwarf and standard budded fruit trees. Wholesale and retail.

Cumberland Valley Nurseries, Inc. (10)
P.O. Box 430
113 Lind Street
McMinnville, TN 37110
Catalog specializing in plums, peaches, and nectarines. Wholesale and retail.

Farmer Seed & Nursery Co. (11)
Faribault, MN 55021
General seed catalog. Flowers, vegetables, fruit, and nursery stock.

Henry Field Seed & Nursery Co. (12)
407 Sycamore Street
Shenandoah, IA 51601
General seed and nursery catalog. Flowers, vegetables, fruit, gardening aids, and nursery stock.

Dean Foster Nurseries (13)
Hartford, MI 49257
General catalog specializing in strawberries. Flowers, vegetables, dwarf fruit, and berries. Wholesale and retail.

Fowler Nurseries, Inc. (14)
525 Fowler Road
Newcastle, CA 95658
Price list of over 200 varieties sent on request. Commercial price list also available. Catalog $1.

Grootendorst Nurseries (15)
Lakewide, MI 49116
Specialists in dwarf Malling and Merton rootstock.

Gurney Seed & Nursery Co. (16)
1448 Page St.
Yankton, SD 57078
General seed catalog. Flowers, vegetables, fruit, and nursery stock.

Haley Nursery Co., Inc. (17)
Smithville, TN 37116
Price list on fruit trees, specializing in peaches and nectarines. Wholesale only. Ask your dealer to order.

Heath's Nursery, Inc. (18)
P.O. Box 707
Brewster, WA 98812
Catalog of fruit, shade, and ornamental trees.

Inter-State Nurseries (19)
Hamburg, IA 51640
Fruit, flowers, berries, roses, and ornamentals.

Ison's Nursery & Vineyard (20)
Brooks, GA 30205
Catalog specializing in grapes. Wholesale and retail.

J. W. Jung Seed Co. (21)
Station 8
Randolph, WI 53956
General seed catalog. Flowers, vegetables, fruit, and nursery stock.

Catalog Sources (continued)

Kelly Bros. Nurseries, Inc. (22)
Dansville, NY 14437
Catalog of fruit, nuts, flowers, and ornamentals.

Lawson's Nursery (23)
Route 1, Box 294
Ball Ground, GA 30107
Fruit catalog specializing in old-fashioned and unusual fruit trees. Lists over 100 varieties of old apples.

Henry Leuthardt Nurseries, Inc. (24)
East Moriches, Long Island, NY 11940
Fruit catalog and guidebook on dwarf and espalier-trained fruit trees.

Earl May Seed & Nursery Co. (25)
Shenandoah, IA 51603
General seed catalog. Flowers, vegetables, fruit, and nursery stock.

Miller's Nursery, Inc. (26)
Canandaigua, NY 14424
Fruit specialists. Catalog also includes garden aids and ornamentals.

New York State Fruit Testing Cooperative Association (27)
Geneva, NY 14456
Fruit catalog. $4 membership fee, refunded on first order.

L. L. Olds Seed Co. (28)
P.O. Box 7790
Madison, WI 53701
General seed catalog. Flowers, vegetables, fruit, and nursery stock.

Owen's Vineyard and Nursery (29)
Georgia Highway 85
Gay, GA 30218
Catalog specializing in muscadine grapes. Includes guidelines for growing and training. Southern rabbiteye blueberries are available.

Rayner's Bros., Inc. (30)
P.O. Box 1617
Salisbury, MD 21801
Fruit catalog specializing in strawberries.

Southmeadow Fruit Gardens (31)
2363 Tilbury Place
Birmingham, MI 48009
Probably the largest collection of fruit varieties, old, new, and rare, in the United States. Illustrated catalog is priced at $5 and worth it. A condensed catalog is free.

Stanek's Garden Center (32)
East 2929 — 27th Avenue
Spokane, WA 99203
Catalog of fruit, berries, flowers, and ornamentals.

Stark Bros. Nursery (33)
Louisiana, MO 63353
Illustrated catalog and guide to vegetables, fruit, nuts, and ornamentals.

Van Well Nursery (34)
P.O. Box 1339
Wenatchee, WA 98801
Fruit and berry catalog. Wholesale and retail.

Waynesboro Nurseries (35)
P.O. Box 987
Waynesboro, VA 22980
Catalog of fruits, nuts, and ornamental plant material.

Weeks Berry Nursery (36)
6494 Windsor Island Road No.
Salem, OR 97303
Specializing in small fruits. Wholesale and commercial plantings.

Dave Wilson Nursery (37)
Box 90 A
Hughson, CA 95326
Fruits, berries, grapes. Specializing in Zaiger patented fruit frees. Wholesale and retail.

H. G. Hastings Co. (38)
Box 4655
Atlanta, GA 30302
General seed catalog. Flowers, vegetables, fruits, and nursery stock.

Bryants Nursery (39)
P.O. Box 422
Helena, GA 31037

Buckley Nursery Co. (40)
Buckley, WA 98321
Catalog of fruit, flowers, and shade and ornamental trees. Wholesale and retail.

Hilltop Orchards & Nurseries, Inc. (41)
Rt. 2
Hartford, MI 49057
Widely recognized fruit tree specialists for commercial orchardists. Free handbook and catalog.

Armstrong Nurseries (42)
P.O. Box 4060
Ontario, CA 91761
Specialists in fruit trees and roses. Catalog lists genetic dwarf peaches and nectarines, as well as other exotic fruit trees. Vegetables and bulbs.

W. F. Allen Co. (43)
P.O. Box 1577 H
Salisbury, MD 21801
Strawberry specialists. Catalog and planting guide lists over 30 varieties. Wholesale and retail.

Mayo Nurseries (44)
Route 14
Lyons, NY 14489
Fruit specialists. Catalog includes many varieties of dwarf and semidwarf apples. Wholesale and retail.

Fruit trees and berry canes combine with ornamental annuals and vegetables to create a productive oasis.

Index

Page numbers in italics indicate illustrations.